THE CLASH

Other titles in the series

THE CLASH

David Quantick

THUNDER'S
MOUTH
PRESS

Published in the United States by
Thunder's Mouth Press
841 Broadway, Fourth Floor
New York, NY 10003

First published in Great Britain by Unanimous Ltd
254–258 Goswell Road, London EC1V 7RL

Series Editor: John Aizlewood
Project Editor: Nicola Birtwisle

Library of Congress Card Number: 99–69758

ISBN: 1–56025–269–3

Printed in Italy

1 2 3 4 5 6 7 8 9

CONTENTS

ACKNOWLEDGEMENTS

I'd like to thank John Aizlewood for asking me to do this book in the first place, and for not going on too much about remix albums and Ellen Foley, and Simon Huxstep for his advice and comments. Anyone interested in reading more about The Clash is directed to Marcus Gray's comprehensive *Last Gang In Town: The Story And Myth Of The Clash* and Johnny Green and Garry Barker's hilarious *A Riot Of Our Own: Night And Day With The Clash*. The *Clash On Broadway* booklet and *The Clash Songbook* also contain good stories about the band, and the internet has hundreds of Clash web sites, some of them superb.

ACKNOWLEDGEMENTS

ONE

THE STORY

In 1976 England had one of its hottest summers ever. England is a cold, damp country full of snot and coughing, so English people tend to get excited when it's warm. And in 1976, when it was very warm, a lot of English people got very excited. All through the summer, fat blue skies radiated boiling heat, the sun shone like a bastard and the reservoirs literally dried up. The government went mad, breaking all traditions of British reserve, and told everyone in the country to save water by showering with a friend. But even before this, in the far-off spring of 1976, things began to warm up.

On April 30, 1976, a four-piece band called The 101'ers, named after the address of the illegally squatted house where the members of the group lived, played a show in London at a sweat-sodden club called The Nashville Rooms, the kind of venue where the carpets are hard and sticky with beer and the smell of men who drink fills every molecule of air. The 101'ers were a competent pub rhythm and blues band with a thing for Chuck Berry riffs. Their greatest asset was that their singer was a 24-year-old ex-busker and R&B fan who'd once called himself Woody, after Bob Dylan's folk-singing hero Woody Guthrie. Now he called himself Joe Strummer. That night in a stinking rock hovel, Joe Strummer's life changed forever, and as a result, so did the lives of thousands more.

Supporting The 101'ers was a new band called The Sex Pistols, who'd been getting a reputation as a shambolic and aggressive live act with a bizarre, confrontational lead singer who had famously been quoted as saying: 'We're not into music. We're into chaos.' For most of Joe Strummer's generation of musicians, The Sex Pistols were a joke, a noisy hype, similar to America's messy glam-rock drug band The New York Dolls; they seemed to be more into their trouble-making image and their bondage trousers than their music, and in 1976, music was very important. Bands who didn't play long guitar solos clearly weren't proper musicians, and so didn't count.

Strummer, however, was more open-minded. In fact, he was deeply impressed by the band even before they played, when he overheard them discussing with their manager what clothes they should be wearing for the show. Such attention to detail was unheard of at a time when most groups shuffled onstage dressed in a thrilling ensemble of denim, cheesecloth and T-shirts. Dress-wise, seeing a band in 1976 was like watching The Brady Bunch with beards and beer guts attempt to bore a room stupid with well-crafted, mind-killing soft rock. Only duller.

The Sex Pistols were very fast, very offensive and none too concerned about playing tastefully and subtly. After they finished their set, Joe Strummer found that he no longer cared deeply about playing old-fashioned rock 'n' roll in a good-time pub band. His whole attitude had been altered by one concert by an unknown band.

And then a few days later a remarkable thing happened. Joe Strummer was approached by a man called Bernard Rhodes, who happened to be an associate of Sex Pistols manager Malcolm McLaren. Rhodes invited Strummer to do the exact thing Strummer had been thinking about: to leave The 101'ers and join a new band. Intrigued, Strummer went along to meet this new ensemble and found it consisted solely of two guitarists. One was a very thin man called Keith Levine, and the other was an obvious rock-star type called Mick Jones. Jones and Levine were looking for a singer and a drummer. They already had a bass player in mind, an attractive young man named Paul Simonon, who couldn't actually play the bass but looked great.

At any other time in music history, Joe Strummer would probably have looked at the two weirdos who were sitting on a bed staring at him and walked out of the room. But it was 1976, he'd just seen a band who were nothing like anyone else, and it was time to make decisions.

'When I met Mick and Keith at the squat,' Strummer recalled later, 'we went in and looked at each other, and Bernie said, "This is the guy you've got to write songs with", and Mick sort of scowled. I thought, "Well I haven't got any choice. This is what I've got to do".'

Strummer said yes, and on May 31, 1976, The Clash were invented.

Of course, history isn't quite that clear-cut. Strummer had been invited to meet Mick Jones because Jones and Paul Simonon had seen The 101'ers play. They were well aware of who Strummer was and admired the way he performed onstage, even if they weren't wild about his band. And Strummer was aware of the other two as well. He'd seen them out and about with, of all people, The Sex Pistols' bass player Glen Matlock. 'As soon as I saw Mick and Paul walking down Ladbroke Grove with Glen Matlock,' he said later, 'I wanted to join The Clash.'

In its lifetime, The Clash's line-up was to go through a few changes. They would lose drummers. They would add keyboard players. They would hire bass players to play the hard bits. They would even sack Mick Jones during the ill-advised Clash Mark II period. But the essential Clash are the trio who appear on the cover of their first album; Strummer, Jones and Simonon. These three divergent personalities would define and mould the sound and, more importantly, the attitude of the band. Significantly, the fact that one of them wasn't a proper musician was as relevant as the fact that the other two had very different visions of 'rock 'n' roll'.

The band's most notable visionary was its main singer, Joe Strummer, who even in 101'ers days was given to extraordinary features of shamen-like rock singer behaviour. The 101'ers single 'Keys To Your Heart' is a poppy R&B tune with a nice chorus and a lyric about, well, owning the keys to someone's heart. Strummer sings the song and then, halfway through, slows it down to nothing to deliver a bizarre and not wholly coherent rant about a 'big blue policeman' and his 'little black book'. Even in 1975, he was a preaching rocker in the Bruce Springsteen mode.

Joe Strummer's life, unsurprisingly, is an unusual one. He once summed up his early career in a rather abrupt manner: 'I was born in Ankara, then I grew up and learned some Woody Guthrie songs. Then I joined the Clash.' But, as you'd expect from an original punk rocker, there are holes in his story (for a movement obsessed with 'the truth', punk was responsible for some of the best lying in the history of music).

Joe Strummer, who claimed to be the 21-year-old son of a 'white collar worker' at the start of punk, was born John Graham Mellor on August 21, 1952 in Ankara, Turkey. His father was a clerical officer in the British Foreign Office who later received the MBE (Member of the British Empire), the same medal awarded to The Beatles. Strummer's family later lived outside London near the unfashionable satellite town of Croydon, and he was educated at a private boarding school, the City of London Freeman's School, where nothing is known about his childhood except that he was apparently a keen stamp collector. After he left school and dropped out of art college in 1970, John Mellor started calling himself Woody and began a new life as the man who passed the hat round for his busker friend Tymon Dogg.

Woody Mellor became a busker himself and played around Europe for a while, and then gave that up and went to live in Wales, where he hung out with local heroes The Rip Off Park Rock 'n' Roll All Stars and actually joined a band himself, The Vultures. In 1974, he moved to London where, as was the fashion, he joined some friends in illegally occupying – squatting – a house in West London. With his housemates, he formed the magnificently-titled El Huaso and the 101 All Stars, a name sadly shortened to just The 101'ers, and chose his latest, best pseudonym, derived from his basic guitar-strumming technique: Joe Strummer.

Things sped up. Ex-busker Woody Mellor was now pub rocker Joe Strummer, singing R&B songs like Them's 'Gloria' and the old New Orleans tune 'Junco Partner', and writing originals with self-explanatory titles like '5 Star Rock 'n' Roll Petrol', 'Letsagetabitarockin' and 'Jail Guitar Doors'. A year later, The 101'ers played the Nashville Rooms, Joe Strummer saw The Sex Pistols, and then he met Mick Jones and Paul Simonon.

Simonon's memory of Strummer at the time is typically cheerful and mocking. 'When Joe came along it was like having a dad in the group. He was like a teacher because he had been in a group before. He's generally patient. He hardly ever gets angry. He's a real laugh.'

Jones, as Strummer noted, merely scowled. But then Mick Jones came from a very different rock 'n' roll background.

Born Michael Geoffrey Jones on June 26, 1955 in Brixton, South London, Mick Jones was raised by his grandmother Stella in West London. He grew up in one of the tower blocks that fill the lyrics of countless British punk rock songs, hung around with bad boys and got into Mott The Hoople, the hard-rocking people's band with a self-referential streak whose biggest fan was David Bowie, who wrote 'All The Young Dudes' for them.

Jones left school with long hair and narrow striped trousers and, in 1974, joined a rock band with New York Dolls tendencies called The Delinquents, who had, if nothing else, a talent for terrible name changes. They renamed themselves Little Queenie in 1975, and then became Violent Luck when they worked with Guy Stevens, Mott The Hoople's original producer and the man who would later produce The Clash's *London Calling*. Perhaps ironically, Stevens advised the band to sack Jones, and Mick went off and formed the legendary pre-punk supergroup with the dubious name, London SS, with future Generation X and Sigue Sigue Sputnik founder Tony James and soon-to-be Damned guitarist Brian James.

Many musicians who were soon to be famous came and auditioned for London SS. Paul Simonon auditioned, but wasn't good enough. Both Clash drummers Terry Chimes and Topper Headon came for jobs. Even Manchester-based New

York Dolls fan Stephen Morrissey applied for a position: by mail, which wasn't a good idea.

Jones left London SS and played with future Pretender Chrissie Hynde and Sex Pistols Glen Matlock and Steve Jones until early 1976. Sadly he ignored Bernie Rhodes's advice and elected not to form a group with Hynde called Big Girl's Underwear. Then – still keeping in contact with Simonon – he decided to form a new band.

His choice of bandmates was an odd one for such a guitar hero. While Keith Levine was a individual guitarist (his later work with Public Image Limited is extraordinary even now), Paul Simonon wasn't even a musician. He was an art student, into painting and movies, who used to play according to differently coloured stickers that Jones had stuck onto his bass guitar.

However, Simonon is a remarkable man, good-looking in a broody way, and so – always important, this – he looked like a rock star. Born Paul Gustave Simonon – he has French ancestors – on December 15, 1955 in South London, he moved to live with his father in West London and then went to art school, where he developed an individual painting style. After his failed audition for London SS, Simonon stayed in touch with Jones. Their life at the time seems to have consisted entirely of either going to see The Sex Pistols and The 101'ers or wandering around West London with various musicians, looking cool and famous. They lacked only one thing: a singer.

Thus, by May 1976, The Clash had a singer, a bass player and a guitarist. They had a couple of songs (including Strummer's 101'ers tune 'Jail Guitar Doors' and Jones's Delinquents tune '1–2 Crush On You'), a great name (having wisely rejected The Phones, The Mirrors, The Outsiders and The Weak Heart Drops), and, in Bernie Rhodes, a manager full of inspired, albeit often elusive, ideas. Now, thanks to Strummer, they even had a slogan. 'The Clash,' Joe Strummer would tell anyone he could get to listen, 'are The Only Band That Matters.'

In June 1976, of course, The Only Band That Matters didn't Matter very much at all, except to Strummer, Jones, Simonon and Rhodes. To make them matter, things had to advance quickly, especially as the McLaren-bankrolled Sex Pistols were getting noticed. Rhodes had access to a railway storage shed in North London's Camden Town, then a grim and grimy area full of awful pubs and scary people that had not yet reinvented itself as a grim and grimy area full of awful street markets and scary tourists. Rhodes gave the space over to The Clash as a rehearsal space with a bizarre name. Years later Mick Jones would speculate about the origins of this name, thinking it might be a Jewish thing; but if that was the case, it would have been called Rehearsals Schmehearsals, not, as Rhodes had it, Rehearsal Rehearsals.

According to Clash legend, Rehearsal Rehearsals was the coldest, darkest, glummest place in the world. The jukebox played reggae and the band played in mittens. The decor was pink and black, the colours of rockabilly and frostbite. The seats were old barber's chairs which came in handy for chopping people's hair up punk-style, and there was a one-bar electric fire, while Simonon's mural of a car dump, tower blocks and the Westway trunk road merely suggested homesickness for West London. And they were hungry: once, after a long night spent putting up posters, Simonon heated up the remainder of the flour and water paste on a rusty blade and ate it.

Simonon's other big artistic influence at the time came, allegedly – The Clash could always turn any incident into a myth – from his painting of the studio. The rest of the band were so impressed by his paint-spattered overalls that they painted their clothes and instruments with random glops of paint. Simonon, in true Clash style, has always denied that this look was derived from the work of painter Jackson Pollock, who painted his canvases in much the same way. This may be true, but it would make Simonon the only art student on Earth who has never heard of Jackson Pollock. They also stencilled slogans stolen from reggae album covers and terrorist group manifestos onto their overalls. This had the dual effect of making them stand out in the street, and, more importantly, giving them an image different from that of the bondage-geared Sex Pistols, a band literally dressed by Malcolm McLaren's partner Vivienne Westwood. Soon The Clash's look changed yet again, to the skinny ties, straight trousers and narrow-lapel jackets that they wore on the cover of the first album. This was a good idea; until now Jones and Simonon had still been making their own clothes from ladies' car coats.

It was around this time that Simonon named the band. Noting the amount of times the word 'clash' appeared in newspaper headlines, he suggested it as a group name. Given the peculiar nature of the British press, The Clash might by this method have easily become The Naughty Vicars or The Three-Way Love Nest. Now that the most important stuff – the look and the attitude – was sorted out, it was time to work on the music. The Clash had as yet no drummer, so auditions were held. Again, Clash myth has it that over 200 drummers auditioned. Among them were Richard Dudanski, once with Strummer in The 101'ers, later of Public Image Limited, who said no, and Pablo Labritain, who became Clash Drummer Number One. He didn't last and went on to join pop punks 999.

The man who took the job was Terry Chimes. Chimes, an East Ender born on June 25, 1955, had passed this way before, auditioning for early Jones bands like Violent Luck and London SS. His attitude was not deeply Clash-like; rather than smashing the system, his ambition was to make enough money to buy an expensive car. However, he was an excellent drummer, and the sound of the early Clash began to crystallise around him.

On Independence Day 1976 The Clash played their first gig. For some reason it wasn't in London but a couple of hundred miles away in the northern steel town of Sheffield, which would one day produce Def Leppard, The Human League and Pulp, but for now was playing unwitting host to an astonishingly significant moment in pop history. That July night, supporting the Sex Pistols, The Clash took the stage for the first time at the Black Swan pub, whose romantic local nickname was the Mucky Duck. No record exists of this concert, but it is known that The Clash's repertoire at this time included 'Deny', 'Protex Blue', 'What's My Name?' and Strummer's rather odd 'How Can I Understand The Flies?', a song which, perhaps understandably, was never recorded by The Clash or indeed anyone. The nature of punk rock meant that meditative, quirky tunes with long, silly names were out, while short, angry songs about lying, identity and sex were in.

In August, an equally significant event in Clash lore occurred. The 1976 Notting Hill Carnival – 20 years after its start as a local event rooted in West London's West Indian community – was heavily policed and turned into a full-scale riot, with police versus black youth in the streets. Local residents Joe Strummer and Paul Simonon had attended, as the event involves a lot of reggae and dope-smoking, and joined in the general aggression against the police, throwing bricks and plastic traffic cones. It was an extraordinarily exciting and dangerous event, and full of punk rock qualities such as anarchy, subversion and political violence. Strummer must have felt that the words of The Clash's songs were coming alive in front of him. The fracas was a direct inspiration to what would become one of The Clash's most misunderstood songs, the powerful and aggressive 'White Riot', whose lyric about black and white attitudes was a little naive (when black people have a problem, do they really just 'throw a brick'?) but whose sentiment was not, as some tried to claim, racist in any way.

The Clash's increasingly political direction led to further developments. The Jones song 'Mark Me Absent' was dropped, possibly for political reasons, while, more significantly, the band's third guitarist Keith Levine left, later saying, 'I wasn't into politics'. In fact he was into heroin, which did not prevent him continuing as a musician. After a period of doing very little (apart, possibly, from smack), he gravitated towards the West London set of John Lydon and Lydon's old friend John 'Jah Wobble' Wardle, where the combination of Lydon's amphetamine use, Wobble's fondness for marijuana and Levine's heroin intake must have made conversation interesting.

With Richard Dudanski, the trio formed Public Image Limited, possibly the most exciting post-punk band. After a galvanising debut single, 'Public Image', in which Lydon attacked either himself or Malcolm McLaren over Wobble's huge bassline and Levine's screaming, grating guitar, the band recorded one self-indulgent album and one utterly brilliant one, *Metal Box*, now called *Second Edition*. Anyone listening to Levine's astonishing guitar now, the sound of metal being ripped – both original and the perfect backdrop for Lydon's twisted and emotive vocals – has to stop and wonder how Levine could have fitted into a band who, at the exact moment *Metal Box* was released, were recording the far more traditional *London Calling*. Later, differences between Levine and Lydon (either drug- or ego-related, but in the end everyone but Lydon has fled PiL) caused him to leave the band and little has been heard from him since.

Meanwhile The Clash's street cred (a phrase that was amazingly popular at the time but seems to have gone the way of all flesh lately) took a great big knocking when Joe Strummer moved out of his squat and into a friend's house. His new friend was Sebastian Conran, son of Terence Conran, the founder of the Habitat store chain. Sebastian had the lease on a very big house in London's Regent's Park, an exclusive part of town where most of the property belonged to The Queen. While there is no law against having posh people for friends, it was considered highly amusing by some at the time that by night Strummer was singing about unemployment and poverty, while by day he was living with a millionaire's son. In fact Sebastian Conran was a hugely valuable asset to the Clash camp; his talents enabled him to design extremely powerful flyers for early Clash and Sex Pistols concerts, using collage imagery and cut-ups from the essential pre-punk sociology book *Folk Devils and Moral Panics*. But, like a hideous mutant child, he was always kept to one side by the band, who couldn't mention him in interviews as even his Christian name was posh.

By now interviews were actually beginning to happen. Nowadays, the British music press is so keen to uncover new talent that a band like Oasis can have a *New Musical Express* front cover before they've even released a single, but in the sluggish '70s, things moved much more slowly. The Clash had to wait until November 1976 to be featured in a piece about 'two new hot punk bands', i.e. The Clash and The Damned, in the world's dullest rock magazine, *Melody Maker*. The interview was conducted by Caroline Coon, who at the time was, rather conveniently, going out with Paul Simonon. The Clash, still London-based, still with no record out, were becoming nationally famous. They continued to write songs for what would become their debut LP, often in a flat punkily situated on the 18th floor of a council high rise on West London's Harrow Road. The flat was owned by Jones's grandmother, who regularly turned up at Clash gigs.

Around this time the producer Guy Stevens came to see The Clash rehearse. Stevens is an important figure in the story of The Clash. He had already been responsible for getting Mick Jones kicked out of The Delinquents, but his other credentials were like catnip to Joe Strummer. In the 1960s, Stevens had stood bail for one of Strummer's heroes, Chuck Berry, had produced The Who, several ska records for Island, and, as we have already noted – of special significance to Jones and Strummer – had produced all the early records by the great British rock band Mott The Hoople, whose self-mythologising and 'people's band' rock 'n' roll approach would be a huge influence on The Clash.

Stevens was impressed with The Clash. 'They were doing 'White Riot' and I just thought, "Right! RIOT! RIGHT! RIOT! Let's goooooh!"' he later told *NME's* Charles Shaar Murray. Stevens recorded 'White Riot', 'Career Opportunities', 'Janie Jones', '1977' and 'London's Burning', which were recorded for Polydor Records. Sadly, Stevens, also an alcoholic with problems, made a hash of the demos – insisting, bizarrely, that Strummer pronounce his consonants properly – and they were never used. The band and Stevens would, however, meet again later, with far more fortunate consequences.

The Clash had their first television interview around this time on the local London Weekend Show, where they were interviewed by Janet Street-Porter, who was later squired by Tony James of – what other band could it be? – London SS, and more recently became editor of national newspaper *The Independent On Sunday*. Things were hotting up, but by now Terry Chimes had had enough of being in The Clash and not agreeing with anyone about anything, so he left the band. Unfortunately, it was the beginning of December and The Clash were about to go out on the most important punk tour of all time, the Anarchy Tour. It was to feature The Clash, The Damned and The Sex Pistols and be a well-regulated tour of the country, enabling people actually to see all the new punk rock bands at first hand. By now, alas, punk's reputation had spread...

In 1976, unlike America and Europe, where there was a large degree of either sexual or economic freedom, Britain was a small penniless island where you couldn't go dancing after midnight, or buy a drink or even watch a television show after 11. Life was very stagnant and, even for the times, seemed somehow out of date. Musically, nothing exciting apart from disco had happened since glam rock some five years before, and politically the country exchanged a dull Labour Prime Minister for a dull Conservative Prime Minister every four years, as if there was a big warehouse behind the House Of Commons that every so often they went into and fetched out a dull old man.

The most thrilling event of the period was scheduled to happen in 1977, the year of the Queen of England's Silver Jubilee, celebrating 25 years of grinding the proletariat's faces into the dirt with an iron heel. Royalty, in the days before Di and Fergie, was a highly respected trade, and people still, amazingly, had a degree of reverence for the Queen and her German relations. The Silver Jubilee – and this punk-loving author is not ashamed to say he proudly displayed a Silver Jubilee badge – was a huge jamboree. People put tables out in the road, draped plastic Union Jacks all over them and drank the monarch's health. For most of the country, it was a time of national unity.

For others, of course, it was a big horrible piece of stinking crap, another symptom of the boring life that surrounded every excitable British teenager. So when the Anarchy Tour set out on its long trek, hundreds of fed-up punk fans – all safety pins and ripped school uniforms – were looking forward to some loud, angry fun. Which is almost certainly why nearly every local council and religious group in the country, influenced by reports of The Sex Pistols' mass swearathon on London's Today television show, decided that the Anarchy Tour was a very bad thing indeed. The Clash found themselves with no dates to play and, instead of forging a national bond with the country's annoyed youth, returned to London for a quiet punk rock Christmas. Musically, this may have been a good thing, as the emerging punk bands had little or no solidarity with one another – Johnny Rotten being particularly down on Joe Strummer, whom he saw as a copycat toff – and the Anarchy Tour might well have descended into bitching and in-fighting at speed.

With the Jubilee on the way and a host of new bands on the Pistols and The Clash's heels, it was clearly going to be a big punk year. The Clash, who had already written a song called '1977', perhaps inspired by the reggae band Culture's Rastafarian apocalypse number 'Two Sevens Clash', began 1977 by playing a New Year show at Central London's brand new, all-punk Roxy club, which was a kind of Studio 54-

cum-Viper Room for the new punk rock elite. Like The Clash, the Roxy's music was a wild mix of reggae and punk, and its DJ was reggae fan and film-maker Don Letts, who was quickly to become a very important associate of The Clash, as late as 1999 putting together their official biopic *From Westway To The World*.

However, the most important event in The Clash's entire career was to occur at the end of January. It's an occasion that is significant in the life of every rock artist, but in the case of The Clash it was an absolutely critical moment. And, since it involved The Clash, it was by no means simple or even sensible.

On January 27, 1977, Bernie Rhodes – apparently taking the band to Polydor Records, whom they were about to sign to – suddenly suggested to the group that they might care to pop into the Soho Square headquarters of the British arm of CBS Records for ten minutes. The Clash followed Rhodes into the building, where they met dog-loving, eccentrically millinered CBS boss Maurice Oberstein, who promptly signed them to the label for a £100,000 advance. In a simple, typically Rhodes-like act, the country's most important unsigned punk band (The Sex Pistols had already released their debut single 'Anarchy In The UK' on EMI, and were currently going through their comic process of trying on every record label in Britain for size) had, within the space of a few minutes, been sold to the record company most associated with Big Corporate Badness, the actual spiritual home of hippy music's sworn fictional enemy, The Man.

The significance of this event outside the band and the devastating effect it had on The Clash's credibility is discussed later, but for the band themselves, the situation did not seem too awful. They shrugged off accusations of selling out from their critics, pointing out that no one could buy their records if they didn't have a record company (the hugely varied British independent record company network of the 1980s simply did not exist at this point), and that their huge-for-the-time advance was for not one or two albums, but an absurd eight.

It was this, not the political ramifications of the deal, that would come to obsess The Clash. Strummer still remembers January 27 with fear and horror. 'I forget my birthday but I never forget that date,' he said, memorably, a few years later. The Clash would spend their entire career regretting the hand-cuffing deal they had signed, even recording a double and a triple album in the mistaken belief that this would get them out of their contract, and it almost certainly contributed to the band's premature demise. For The Clash, CBS would come to be some kind of arch-enemy, and its American arm Epic a permanent stranglehold. On the other hand, if they had signed to Stiff, they'd never have written 'Complete Control'.

Meanwhile, Polydor Records' Chris Parry (soon to manage The Cure), who'd been rather looking forward to signing The Clash, was alerted to a new band called The Jam by punk face-about-town Shane MacGowan (later of punk band The Nipple Erectors and much later of The Pogues), so he signed them instead, giving the world the thoughts and work of the always-reliable Paul Weller.

The Clash were now very ready to go into the studio and actually make a record. The Sex Pistols already had ('Anarchy In The UK'), The Damned had ('New Rose', the first punk single), and even Manchester's Buzzcocks, who formed after seeing The Sex Pistols, had released an EP, 'Spiral Scratch', on the tiny New Hormones label, one of the first truly independent records. Things were moving swiftly along, and CBS were keen for the band to record 'White Riot'. Unfortunately The Clash had no drummer. Someone called Rob Harper was asked back, and they also auditioned Jon Moss.

Moss is one of the strangest figures in punk rock. He achieved fame in the 1980s as the drummer in Culture Club. Oddly for a drummer, he was an opinionated man whose right-wing views were at odds with most of the kneejerk liberal opinions of most bands, but they fitted in rather well with the Thatcher/Reagan era. Moreover, real notoriety came in the 1990s when every interview Boy George gave seemed to be about their love affair.

Moss was one of the few punk musicians to be totally honest about his wealthy background and disdain for anarchist politics. Captain Sensible of The Damned was deeply fond of telling people that, when Moss had been The Damned's drummer, the band went round to see him and his door was opened by a butler. The idea of The Clash – the most left-wing and militant group of 1976 – auditioning a man who was, in many ways, the embodiment of the coming Thatcher '80s, is to some a really exciting one. The Clash with Jon Moss as drummer would have been something like REM with the editor of *Forbes* magazine on bass.

In the end The Clash unwittingly began one of their less-well-known traditions: they invited Terry Chimes to return. In February, having recorded 'White Riot' and its B-side, '1977', The Clash commenced sessions for the album proper.

One of the first songs recorded for the album was the exciting 'I'm So Bored With The USA', which seems to have been musically inspired by The Sex Pistols' 'Pretty Vacant', with its shouty chorus and jangly introduction, and which had become much more of a political number in the past few months, the also-rewritten 'What's My Name?' and a cover version of Junior Murvin's soon-to-be reggae classic 'Police And Thieves'.

'Police And Thieves', more than anything else on *The Clash*, was an important song for the band. Distinguishing them from every other punk band – none of whom had attempted anything like a full-blown cover of a genuine reggae song at this point (white reggae covers being the province of Eric Clapton and bawdy singer Judge Dread at the time) – the story also showed Jones's originality as an arranger, as he instructed Strummer to crash his guitar shockingly on every other beat.

The other very significant song was 'Garageland', the band's official manifesto, based on Charles Shaar Murray's famous *NME* review that suggested the band should be returned to the garage with the engine still running. 'Garageland' has been criticised as a song which mythologises The Clash, who didn't play in any garages when they started and would not play in any later on, but the point of the song is that it acted as a magnet and a manifesto for hundreds of other bands, who did form in garages. 'Deny' and 'Cheat' obeyed the punk law; write as many songs about liars as you can, while 'White Riot' (under the other punk law that said you couldn't have your single on the album, and if you did, it had to be a different version) was a remix of a demo, long touted as a 'live' version.

On March 18, the single version of 'White Riot' was released in Britain in an attractive sleeve depicting Strummer, Simonon and Jones up against a wall, a pose taken from the sleeve of a dub LP called *State Of Emergency* by Joe Gibbs & The Professionals. It received no airplay whatsoever, other than exposure on late-night alternative shows, particularly Radio One's John Peel Show. This blanket – and deliberate – ignoring of the song inspired Strummer and Clash cohort Roadent to go out with spray cans and paint the song's name on the windows of London's commercial radio station Capital

Radio and on the doors of the BBC's radio headquarters Broadcasting House. It also inspired the song 'Capital Radio'.

Nowadays all this kind of thing may seem a bit petty, but in the late 1970s, British radio was a horrible, closed mausoleum where new bands might occasionally crawl in like mice and die of starvation in the dark. Radio One in particular, governed by a playlist of iron, saw itself as a 'fun' station, and devoted most of its airtime to either perfectly good pop music and disco, which people wanted, and – lest we forget – still want, to hear, or the worst adult-oriented rock music of all time.

There is little evidence of a history of bribery and payola in British music, but it can be argued that Radio One needed no financial incentive to play bad guitar-based drivel all day and all night long. Worse, there were no evening shows to cater for minority tastes. This situation was to be altered in the wake of punk, but not much. Genuinely popular bands like The Clash, The Sex Pistols and even the more DJ-friendly The Jam were to be denied airtime throughout their careers, a situation which would exist for new British guitar bands until the tiresome advent of Britpop in the 1990s, when Radio One decided that a wave of music based on 1960s guitar pop was right up their street.

Another influence on The Clash's lack of chart success was more self-induced. There were very few outlets for music on television at the time. No real pop video industry meant no MTV, VH-1 or Box, while there were no hip chat shows or trendy kids' programmes. Variety shows would, at best, feature a 'family' act, and the only other options were regional shows, which were watched by a few thousand people, or the two national music shows. One was called, unbelievably, The Old Grey Whistle Test, and was hosted by an ex-policeman called 'Whispering' Bob Harris, who hated modern music (after The New York Dolls had appeared on the show, he dismissed them with the words 'mock rock', thereby endearing The New York Dolls to the nation). This show featured album tracks and live performances, and specialised in very much unpunk acts like Little Feat, Jackson Browne and The Eagles.

The other, more influential, show was Top Of The Pops, a programme which almost automatically guarantees an appearance for any band whose record has recently entered the sales-based UK charts. The Clash qualified for the programme on several occasions, but they refused to appear because at that time bands did not play live on the show. Playing live, here meaning being real and honest, was very important to The Clash, who would later make videos rather than appear on the evil, dishonest, popular Top Of The Pops. This was a brave decision, but one that effectively reduced their chance of being seen by the people they wished to reach – namely, everyone in the country – to roughly nil.

Nevertheless, the music press – at the time selling enough papers to genuinely influence a section of the public – loved The Clash. 'White Riot' was made Single Of The Week in several papers, and the *New Musical Express* even went as far as to release their own Clash single, an interview-cum-music EP which featured the otherwise unavailable tracks 'Capital Radio' and 'Listen', an instrumental that Simonon famously could not play live.

If 'White Riot' had an impact with people who wanted something new from music, then the release on April 8 of the band's debut album, *The Clash*, was even more powerful. From its sleeve (defiant-looking punk trio, charging riot police with truncheons visible, Terry Chimes cruelly credited as Tory

Crimes) to its loud, furious content, *The Clash* is an album that most people prefer to the angrier, nastier and possibly more sincere Sex Pistols debut album *Never Mind The Bollocks...Here's The Sex Pistols*. It may be the best punk debut album, although Buzzcocks' breathtaking *Another Music In A Different Kitchen* offers another, equally exciting side of punk. Certainly the critics were thrilled.

Mark Perry, who produced the first punk fanzine *Sniffin' Glue* (and went on to form South London punk pioneers Alternative TV, a sometimes great band) announced in an upper-case review IT'S AS IF I'M LOOKING AT MY LIFE IN A FILM, and many people felt the same way. Even those who didn't suffer from unemployment, alienation, the dishonesty of others and a general sense of creeping rage soon began to, almost in sympathy, as this very powerful album dug its way into the national consciousness and climbed the British charts to the Number 12 position. Naturally, *The Clash* wasn't released in America, although it did manage to sell a staggering 100,000 copies on import.

Part of the reason for the album's success was that, despite the lack of airplay, it could be promoted through live performance. Now The Clash had, finally, a full-time drummer, Nicky Bowen 'Topper' Headon. Born May 30, 1955 in Bromley, Kent, Headon had been a drummer in a variety of bands and had auditioned for several others, including London SS (and The Clash themselves) before meeting Mick Jones for a third time and receiving an invitation to go on tour with the band. Legend has it that Headon was the 204th drummer auditioned by The Clash and that the band liked Topper because he hit the drums really hard. He probably didn't tell them that his favourite drummer was Phil Collins.

Headon's skills were to come in handy very soon. On

May 9 the first utterly successful major punk concert took place at the Rainbow Theatre in Finsbury Park, North London. The Clash headlined, and were the first punk band to do so. Despite its non-arena status, the Rainbow always had a reputation far larger than its seating capacity, and The Clash were almost overwhelmed to be playing there. The show, the first night of the White Riot Tour, was an extraordinary event. As the Rainbow was a seated venue, and everyone in the audience wanted to dance, pogo or just walk about looking hard, people began to rip the cinema-style seating out and pass it up onto the stage, like bizarre offerings to some punk rock chair god. Despite the lack of violence at the show, The Clash got their first tabloid headline in *The Sun* newspaper – PUNK WRECK.

By now The Clash were attracting the attention of more than the media. Band members were arrested for painting the group's name on a wall, for stealing pillows from a hotel on tour and, weirdest of all, shooting pigeons. Simonon and Strummer had acquired air guns and liked to pose and prance about with them. On one occasion, they decided to shoot some nearby pigeons. Unfortunately, these pigeons were not the common vermin of the air who use London as a giant toilet, but expensive racing pigeons. Worse than that, the pigeons were being kept on railway property, and when the police were called, they decided to treat the offence as terrorism-related. Finally, Strummer had achieved the political martyrdom he liked to flirt with. Or he might have done, had he not been bailed out of jail a few hours later. This all seemed to have a direct bearing on a later, silly, song, 'Guns On The Roof', which is ostensibly about right-wing terrorists, but in reality appears to have been inspired by the pigeon incident, something the band would often deny. This denial was rather spoiled by Strummer's habit of cooing whenever he announced 'Guns On The Roof' onstage.

Even Bernie Rhodes, who once had the license plate CLA 5H, became odder. When American writer Lester Bangs toured England with The Clash that year, Rhodes tried to set him on fire.

Meanwhile, more serious events were occurring. On May 13, CBS released 'Remote Control' as a single without consulting the band. As The Clash had talked about artistic control as one of the few concessions they'd got from CBS, this event made them look a bit silly, particularly as the theme of 'Remote Control' itself was the lack of freedom in modern society. Now The Clash, for all their posturing, were beginning to look like just another CBS band, who could be told what to do by their record company. Rhodes and the band kicked up a stink, citing politics and integrity as a basis for their annoyance, although it would appear that the real reason for their annoyance was simply that the band had wanted the far snappier 'Janie Jones' as the first single from the album. They were right too, for 'Janie Jones' is one of the great lost Clash singles.

While 'Remote Control' failed to chart and inspired nothing but bad feeling between band and label, it did lead directly (as we shall see) to one of the most extraordinary and exciting events in punk, and, even, rock history, an event which, ironically, could never have taken place if The Clash had signed to a small independent label. Incensed and deeply annoyed, The Clash – now with Topper Headon as a full band member – decided that the subject of the follow-up single to 'Remote Control' would be 'Remote Control' itself, or rather the recent disaster its release had caused. Thus on September 23, after a bizarre but creative recording session with the world's most eccentric producer, Lee 'Scratch' Perry – which inspired the Bob Marley & The Wailers song 'Punky Reggae Party' and let The Clash to become the first white band to have their likenesses painted onto the wall of Perry's famous Black Ark recording studios in Jamaica – The Clash released one of the greatest singles of all time, the roaring, furious and intelligent 'Complete Control'.

'Complete Control' was something unique for the times, and is special even now. With the odd exception like The Beatles' extremely self-obsessed 'Ballad Of John And Yoko' or The Sex Pistols' childish but fun 'EMI', pop singles rarely commented directly on actual events. Even the more political classics of the 1960s, such as Marvin Gaye's 'What's Going On', or Bob Dylan's 'A Hard Rain's A-Gonna Fall', were never particularly specific in their accusations, while records like Paul McCartney's 'Give Ireland Back To The Irish' or Dylan's 'Hurricane' were specific but political in a more traditional way.

'Complete Control' was different to these singles because it called attention to a very recent event in the life of the people singing it and offered a criticism of that event which didn't just attack the bad guy (CBS) but also implicated the good guys (The Clash) for their naivety and gullibility. Better than that, it then went on to mock both band and music industry for, respectively, stifling creativity and believing in the myth of rock (when Strummer shouts 'You're my guitar hero!', for once he isn't entirely braying the praises of The Clash). And when he shouts, 'I don't trust you/Why should you trust me?', he's encapsulating the entire relationship between band and label, employer and employee, in one line, that then ends in a great mucous Strummer roar of 'Heugggh!' 'Complete Control' did not, oddly, cause CBS Records to collapse and its staff to bring down capitalism with guns and knives, but it did establish The Clash as more than this year's loud yob band. And better records were to come.

At the end of the year Jones and Strummer went to Jamaica, their would-be spiritual home, to hang out. Simonon did not go, a decision he apparently regrets to this day. It was immensely to the pair's credit that instead of thinking they would be accepted as fellow black people in the guise of white rock stars, they soon realised that they were completely out of place and, according to Jones, only stayed alive because they were mistaken for merchant seamen. Strummer used the experience for the song 'Safe European Home', which, in classic Strummer fashion, is completely honest about its subject matter while at the same time managing to make it sound exciting and romantic.

1977 ended with some success for The Clash and was, with hindsight, one of their best years. They had released two superb singles and an awesomely good LP, they'd beaten both the Curse Of The Clash Drummer and the stigma of Tours That Never Happened, managing to play some of the best punk concerts yet. They'd learned a lot and, most importantly, they'd survived. At the beginning of 1978 The Sex Pistols were effectively over as a group, Lydon walking out of the band's last show in San Francisco.

Other groups were emerging, but with The Jam foundering badly on bad singles and LPs, The Damned splitting up for a while and The Stranglers becoming increasingly unhip, The Clash found themselves undisputed rulers of the big punk bands, a situation which almost instantly came very close to unravelling when CBS released the next single.

'Clash City Rockers', which had started life a year or so back as 'You Know What I Think About You', was not from the album and had been chosen by the band as a single. The problem this time was the actual record itself. Released on February 17, it had been produced and mixed by the first album's producer Mickey Foote while the band were absent. 'Clash City Rockers' sounds muddy and dull, especially after the superb 'Complete Control'. Worse, however, Foote, finding the song a bit sluggish, had sped up the backing track. As one of the great cornerstones of punk was honesty and lack of deception, this was a very bad thing indeed, and may have brought back memories of the first Damned album, which, according to rumour, had been sped up by its producer Nick Lowe to make it sound more punk. Strummer demanded that Foote be sacked, and he never worked with The Clash again.

Punk rock ironies began to build up all around the band. Strummer, fed up with being mocked for living in a 'white mansion' with the son of a toff, moved out into a squat. Meanwhile Jones, who didn't care about this kind of criticism, moved into what was described as 'a rock star flat', full of luxury, stereo systems and mirrors. It was at this time that Jones's rather unmanly hair and distinctly prima-donna-ish persona earned him the nickname in the Clash camp of Poodle.

1978 was a year full of new Clash events. Strummer sent the Northern Irish fanzine *Alternative Ulster* a consignment of lawnmower parts as a thank-you present. More extravagantly, he later gave the unemployment-hit steel town of Corby, Northamptonshire, a pink Cadillac. Not entirely untypically, it was delivered but did not work. The band played on the new British youth television show Something Else, where Strummer suggested that band managers should be put in concentration camps. Mick Jones played on an Elvis Costello record, 'Big Tears', the B-side of 'Pump It Up'. Strummer became violently opposed to the punk practice of spitting at bands, known as gobbing, after someone managed to spit down his throat and he got hepatitis, which led to the cancelling of recording sessions in February 1978.

The sessions resumed in March. Simonon legendarily and hiply became so bored that he asked for war films to be projected on the studio wall. These were not happy times, and even the arrival of the record's producer did not go too well. Sandy Pearlman, best known for his work with the surrealist heavy metal band Blue Oyster Cult, had been chosen by CBS to give The Clash a sound more suited to American radio (by now there were enough new wave and punk records out there for even the dimmest record company to get an idea of how things should sound) and he decided the best place to meet the band would be backstage before a show. Unfortunately, The Clash were not keen to make new friends a few seconds before they went onstage and Pearlman's persistent attempts to get into the dressing room so annoyed one of the band's crew that he knocked Pearlman to the ground. The band, instead of helping him up, simply walked over him on their way out.

This may be the real reason *Give 'Em Enough Rope* sounds so bad. Joe Strummer's voice is mixed cruelly low. The album starts crisp and ends muddy. But as a rule, it's The Clash who make this a bad record, not Pearlman, who simply gave the band a far punchier sound, at the expense of their humanity. The songs, wrapped up in a clean, loud, American-sounding production, are generally of insufficient quality to stand up to this robust treatment. Tunes are poor, songs seem half worked out and the lyrics are frequently ludicrous. There is far too much myth-making going on, from Strummer's absurd trio of 'Last Gang In Town', 'Cheapskates' and 'All The Young

Punks (New Boots And Contracts)' to Jones's tale of school-mates turned jailbirds, 'Stay Free', which at least had a top tune and a splendid guitar solo. *Give 'Em Enough Rope* is an annoying record for anyone not actually in The Clash.

1978 was rapidly turning into a terrible year for The Clash. By now they had been approached with a view to being the featured punk band in a film called *Rude Boy*, which was to centre around the various political happenings around Jubilee year and would focus on The Clash's relationship with one of their real-life fans, a right-wing oaf called Ray Gange. The Clash were asked to improvise important scenes and this, combined with Gange's by-no-means-brilliant philosophising, resulted in an unintentionally funny film. The Clash were quick to denounce the film, largely for one scene depicting black people as pickpockets, but its specially staged concert scenes produced some of the best live footage of the band. The soundtrack remains unreleased, although, happily, John Peel played the whole thing one night on Radio One, to the immense satisfaction of home tapers. At the film's premier, tempers ran so high that one of the directors, Dave Mingay, was punched in the face by a gossip columnist.

Undercurrents of dissatisfaction boiled up so much by the end of the year that on October 21, Bernie Rhodes was sacked. 'I took them off the street and made them what they are,' he declared in a typically self-deprecating press statement.

Rhodes, who would return to the band after working with both The Specials (who began their first hit 'Gangsters' with the line 'Bernie Rhodes knows, don't argue', by which time rancour had already set in) and Dexys Midnight Runners in their early careers, was and is a charismatic figure. Unassuming in appearance, his image problem has always been that he seemed to be slightly but permanently behind Malcolm McLaren, a Stone Temple Pilots to McLaren's Pearl Jam, whereas in reality he was as much at the creative forefront as the Pistols' manager and has never made an opera record or stood for Mayor Of London.

In the interim period before finding a new manager, The Clash decided to manage themselves. In December 1978 they played a benefit show for Sid Vicious's legal fees and went out on the optimistically christened Sort It Out tour. They recorded the first material of their new direction, the blandly poppy 'Cost Of Living' EP, which came out at an unfortunately high price given its name, and was full of songs that one way or another looked to America for inspiration.

1979 was a great year. The Clash embarked on their first American tour. In England, they were Yankophiles supreme, but in America, remembering that they were very punk by the standards of Toto and their ilk, they went the other way. They named their tour Pearl Harbour '79 and opened each show with 'I'm So Bored With The USA'. In July, Epic, noticing perhaps for the first time that The Clash had been to America, and also noticing that the first LP was selling very well on import, decided to release the wrong version, a punk rock mess which got good reviews but was not the album The Clash had recorded. They did, however, actually manage to release a single by The Clash for the first time, 'I Fought The Law', a nice oldie from the 'Cost Of Living' EP.

The Clash now progressed through Britain on their American-named The Clash Take The Fifth tour, accompanied by their new PR, Kosmo Vinyl (not his real name) who introduced them to Ian Dury & The Blockheads. While Dury's appeal, being a funky Cockney who was half music-hall and half surrealist, would always be a very English one, his band were able to play further afield, and Blockhead organist Mickey Gallagher began to play on stage as The Fifth with The Clash (while bassist Norman Watt-Roy and saxophonist Davey Payne would make more clandestine appearances on Clash records). It was around this time that Ian Dury & The Blockheads once turned up unexpectedly at a Clash recording session dressed as policemen (having just appeared on television performing their ironic hit 'I Want To Be Straight'), causing Mick Jones to flush all his illicit substances down the toilet as the rest of the band fled. It was also around this time that The Clash began to be managed by Andrew King and Peter Jenner, who had managed Pink Floyd and would manage Clash-influenced political pop star Billy Bragg.

In October the band recorded two songs for release as singles, the brilliant reggae cover 'Armagideon Time' and Mick Jones's excellent soul pastiche 'Train In Vain', which was to come out as an *NME* single in the manner of 'Capital Radio', but ended up on the next Clash album, *London Calling*. *London Calling* is, almost certainly, the best Clash album, an LP that combined the band's new-found knowledge of America and American culture with a uniquely British approach.

On the one hand hearkening to several musical traditions, on the other looking forward into a grim political reality, the album owes much of its strength to the band's newly regained musical confidence, and to its producer, Guy Stevens. Stevens was still a madman. He would pour beer into a piano to get a better sound, he waved ladders at Mick Jones and, so Strummer claims, he hypnotised the former Woody into writing a song about Montgomery Clift, 'The Right Profile'. While some have tried to downplay Stevens's actual influence on the record, the fact remains that no other Clash record sounds as good as this, as warm and confident and full of energy. It remains, if nothing else, an imaginative peak for The Clash. Reviews were generally favourable, and the band were at a creative highpoint.

1980 saw a brand new Clash plan, what Strummer called The Clash Singles Bonanza. The band were going to release a single every month. Instead, they didn't. The first of the bonanza singles, the reggaefied 'Bankrobber', was halted by CBS, so The Clash went on tour instead. The 16 Tons Tour was not a great success.

I saw it on 15 February at the Electric Ballroom in Camden Town, North London. They weren't very good. In fact, it was such a grim affair that we stood outside the venue after the show and discovered that none of us could agree what songs The Clash had performed. But I still remember the incredible force of the show's opening as Strummer, Jones and Simonon charged out onto the stage, hammering at their guitars like maniacs. I can remember Strummer's impotent fury as he stopped the show to complain about gobbing, and a pleasantly ramshackle version of 'Bankrobber' with Tex-Mex support act Joe Ely accompanying The Clash on accordion.

The Clash went back to America, where they were now even more critically loved after the release of *London Calling* in January 1980. In America, *London Calling* sold 650,000 copies and its single 'Train In Vain' went to Number 23 in the American charts. The band began recording in New York for the first time, doing a fine version of Eddy Grant's 'Police On My Back'. Amazingly, Mick Jones met Joe Strummer's old busking partner Tymon Dogg in the street, and the band recorded Dogg's 'Lose This Skin' with him. Both would appear on *Sandinista!*, the next album.

The band toured Europe and finally forced CBS into releasing 'Bankrobber'. It did not, as the company seemed to expect, end their career, but reached Number 12 in the UK after sales of a Dutch import version woke the label up. America called once more. The British press had started to notice The Clash's secret affair with that country. They recorded not only most of *Sandinista!*, but an album with Mick Jones's girlfriend, Ellen Foley. Her *Spirit Of St Louis* features playing from The Clash, Norman Watt-Roy, Mickey Gallagher, Davey Payne and Tymon Dogg, and is very odd.

In October, a book about The Clash was published. Appropriately enough, it was a book of photos by the excellent photographer Pennie Smith. *The Clash: Before & After* is, inevitably, one of the sexiest rock books, for The Clash were highly image-conscious and look fantastic in black and white. Smith's book gave new force to The Clash, and made them somewhat iconic. It set in concrete the association between the band and the USA. Its captions, written by the band, suggested that The Clash even had a hitherto undetectable sense of humour.

Then, on December 12, 1980, *Sandinista!* emerged, as a 36-song triple album designed unsuccessfully to reduce the amount of albums the band were contracted to make with CBS. It received lashings of bad press, being messily produced, short of good songs, seemingly very indulgent and, of course, far, far too long. All these things are true; however, it should be pointed out that *Sandinista!* came out less than a year after *London Calling* and the band, insanely, and perhaps goaded by their singles ban (just the one single in 12 months, instead of 12), had managed to record five LPs-worth of material in a year. No-one else has ever done this, not even Gerry & The Pacemakers or Beck. With this level of productivity, there was bound to be a slight downturn in quality.

More seriously, Topper Headon's use of heroin was on the increase. He had even begun to use it in the studio, and his health was beginning to suffer. Management team King and Jenner, who had attempted to tell The Clash to do something about Headon's problem, now parted company with the band, who began working with Kosmo Vinyl. Their new tour was called off and CBS, just to make things officially worse, released 'Hitsville UK' as a single, an all-time artistic low.

Joe Strummer, seeing the drift of The Clash's career, threatened to leave the band if Bernie Rhodes wasn't asked back. Rhodes was duly asked back, causing the first major ruction between Strummer, who wanted him, and Jones, who didn't. They immediately set up first a European tour in April, and then a New York residency in May and June. Headon – who had already been charged for drug possession – collapsed after coming off stage on the first night of the European tour, and oversold New York dates actually caused mini-riots in Times Square, forcing the band to extend their residency by a further nine nights. Very punk rock.

By the time of these dates, The Clash were an American band *in excelsis*. Already obsessed with Vietnam through Francis Ford Coppola's *Apocalypse Now*, they were equally into Michael Herr's Vietnam book *Dispatches*, and they were dressed more and more as military types, although contemporary film shows Jones dressed as a poncho-clad cowboy. For support acts the band put on Grandmaster Flash & The Furious Five, who were pelted with rubbish by morons. Graffiti artist and rapper Futura 2000 sprayed and played onstage, and ancient beat poet Allen Ginsberg also came and recited. The Clash had always reneged on their promise to start their own London club, but for sixteen nights in 1981, they had a club, albeit on the wrong continent.

Returning to London, with Headon heavily into heroin, The Clash released another dud single, 'This Is Radio Clash', which was padded out with awful remixes. The Clash did residencies in Paris and London, and Headon was fined £500 for smuggling heroin into Heathrow Airport.

Strummer decided it was time to make a new album. He announced this to Jones, who said he would only do it if it was in New York. The recording of the LP, provisionally entitled *Rat Patrol From Fort Bragg*, was not a happy event. Strummer and Jones worked in separate studios and the album was still not completed in early 1982, recording taking place as the band toured the world. By the time the band hired veteran rock producer Glyn Johns, everything was about to go wrong.

Bernie Rhodes told Strummer it might be a good idea to go missing as a publicity stunt. Strummer decided to make this more authentic, and on April 21, went to Paris without telling Rhodes. Genuine panic ensued and the tour was cancelled. Meanwhile, farcically, Strummer ran in the Paris marathon, presumably staying in the middle where no one could see him, or possibly wearing a chicken costume.

On May 14, with Strummer still absent, the band's fifth album, *Combat Rock*, came out, to mixed reviews – it's a messy but also polite record – and immense sales. Strummer reappeared on May 20. That day, Topper Headon left the band, his drug problems making it impossible for the group to retain him. He was replaced by – who else? – Terry Chimes, who joined the band for a sell-out tour of American stadiums and an appearance on Saturday Night Live, where The Clash promoted 'Should I Stay Or Should I Go?'

That single did OK, but the follow-up, 'Rock The Casbah' – written by Headon and Strummer – reached Number 7 in the

American charts. The Clash had never been so successful, or so in trouble. They spent most of 1983 quietly – Strummer running the London Marathon – and emerged only to play the huge US '83 Festival on May 28 with new drummer Pete Howard. The Clash were paid $500,000 and demanded that the Californian organisers give $10,000 to charity. Then on September 10, the band – or at least two of them – released a press statement. It said, 'Joe Strummer and Paul Simonon have decided that Mick Jones should leave the group.' Tired of Jones's petulance and rock starriness, and probably also just tired of being The Clash, Strummer and Simonon had decided to end the band Jones and Simonon had formed.

The reasons have never been discussed in depth by ex-members of The Clash, but 1999's television/video documentary *From Westway To The World* hints fairly powerfully at the cause, as does ex-road manager Johnny Green's memoir *A Riot Of Their Own*: Mick Jones was a big pain in the ass. Strummer compares him, unfavourably, to Elizabeth Taylor. Green records instances of rock star behaviour (Jones even once told Green to put a cigarette in his mouth before going onstage). Simonon, as a non-songwriter, was unable to work when Jones and Strummer weren't co-operating with each other. Now, Jones claims he has learned 'self-control', always a virtue hard to come by if one is a successful rock musician in America and full of drugs and sex. Strummer, always a more puritan, driven performer, had less time for Jones's rock-star view of life; Simonon, who was all image but also all charm, must have found Jones's attitude intolerable.

Jones, hurt but galvanised into activity, formed a new group, the rock-dance band Big Audio Dynamite. Unwisely, Strummer and Simonon formed a new Clash, with Pete Howard, Nick Sheppard and Vince White, who were apparently asked to turn up to rehearsals and work on tapes of song structures, often without either Strummer or Simonon present. The Clash Mark II's only album, *Cut The Crap*, is a mess, albeit an underrated one, with bizarre production (from Bernie Rhodes, apparently) and some strange songs indeed.

In March 1984, Joe Strummer's father died. Around this time, Johnny Green went to see the new Clash. He told Strummer that the new band was rubbish. Strummer said, 'I know.' The band did a busking tour, which Strummer enjoyed, but not so much that he didn't go and ask Jones to rejoin the band. Jones made up with Strummer, and then played him his new album. Strummer said it was 'shit', and walked out.

On November 23, 1985, the new members of the band were asked to leave, and The Clash were gone forever.

The Clash's solo years have been variable. Topper Headon's has been the saddest life. After the release of his solo album, *Waking Up*, in 1986, Topper was arrested again for drug offences and this time got 15 months in jail for supplying. He continued to have drug problems into the 1990s, despite going into rehab on several occasions, often with Jones and Strummer's financial backing.

Paul Simonon married Tricia Ronane and formed his own band, Havana 3AM, who received no good reviews and split up shortly after recording their one album. He now does well as a painter and has also appeared on a Laura Ashley calendar.

Mick Jones had the most successful early career. Big Audio Dynamite became a hugely popular band, the first to successfully use sampling technology and mix dance music with rock. Sadly, Jones contracted near-fatal pneumonia in 1988; he made a complete recovery and continues to record with the latest version of BAD II today.

Joe Strummer has had the most varied career. For many years, he avoided forming a proper band – in 15 years he has only released two non-soundtrack solo albums – and has involved himself in almost nothing but side projects. For a while he lived in Arizona, and has now returned to England, living in the far-from-urban town of Bridgwater in rural Somerset with his second wife Lucinda.

Strummer, who admits he took on minor projects as a kind of therapy, has appeared in several films, mostly bad ones by maverick director Alex Cox. He plays a bearded dishwasher who gets thrown into a river in Cox's *Walker*. He is seen at length in *Straight To Hell*, kicking a tin can and calling out the names of soccer players David Speedie, Pat Nevin, and Kerry Dixon. And he is good as an expat rockabilly in Jim Jarmusch's *Mystery Train*, where he does an impression of the robot in *Lost In Space*. He gave great interviews, once telling *NME*, 'I've smoked so much pot, I'm surprised I haven't turned into a bush' and he toured with Shane MacGowan's Pogues as well as producing their *Hells' Ditch* album in 1990.

Most of all, bona fide solo albums *Earthquake Weather* and *Rock Art And The X-Ray Style* apart, Strummer has contributed to film soundtracks, generally one or two pieces per film, but on *Walker*, he did some of his best ever work over a soundtrack which was his in its entirety. In 1999, Strummer formed a new band, The Mescaleros, and returned to live work, where he performs 'Straight To Hell', 'London Calling', 'Safe European Home' and others in his set.

Strummer emerged from his vaguely splendid isolation to find that the cynicism and even anger that had greeted his previous musical outings had pretty much dissipated. While his tour with The Clash Mark II had been seen as a feeble attempt to revive a fat smelly corpse with false teeth, his tour with The Mescaleros (a band who could have easily been The Clash Mark II in age and looks) was seen as a lovely return to form. While many, including me, found it as much of a nostalgia jaunt as a tour by The Sex Pistols or The Bootleg Beatles, several saw it as a shining return to form. Opinions differ, but certainly Strummer's taste in Clash songs was impeccable. But given that, for once, a 1970s punk rocker had a new album full of genuinely good, un-nostalgic songs to play, it seemed a shame that Strummer was playing to the punk rock gallery, and an ageing gallery at that. A friend remarked that, as in the old days, all the skinheads were down the front , but this time they were skinheads because they were 40 and all their hair had fallen out. With luck, Strummer will continue to make solo albums that reflect his current musical interests, albums that, while not being a million miles from The Clash's spirit, are clearly not The Clash.

The Clash continue to exist in various forms. In 1991, thanks to a jeans advertisement, 'Should I Stay Or Should I Go?' became a Number One hit single in the UK, the band's first. And in 1999, the band released *From Here To Eternity*, a popular live album, and a slightly biased career retrospective video (directed by Don Letts), *From Westway To The World*. They still, admirably, have no plans to re-form, making them the only major punk band other than Siouxsie & The Banshees who haven't.

On CD, vinyl and video, The Clash can still be seen to be The Only Band That Matters.

TWO

THE MUSIC

While in Britain, The Clash's battles with their record company CBS were at least that – battles – and they were able to at least dispute and comment on record company actions (see 'Complete Control' for details), the situation with their American label Epic was completely different.

Not since the 1960s, when Capitol contrived to take Beatles albums and make their own completely different versions, has a group been so bizarrely served by its record company as The Clash. The Beatles, however, at least saw their early records actually appear in America. The Clash's first eight – eight! – singles weren't released there at all, the first album didn't appear until after their second (and even then tracks were left off to make room for early singles) and the singles 'London Calling', 'Bankrobber' and 'The Call-Up' weren't released at all in America. Epic instead opted to release the insanely bad 'Hitsville U.K.', whose lyrics about the British independent record scene doubtless made a lot of sense in Ohio, Nevada and Louisiana.

Epic then went crazy, respecting the band's wishes and

releasing albums without tinkering with them (and thereby killing *Sandinista!*'s chances of being a hit by not editing it down to a proper single album) and then – just to confuse most of the North American continent – releasing no less than three versions of 'Should I Stay Or Should I Go?', one with Ronald Reagan on the cover, the communist devils. Finally The Clash Mark I split up and Epic declined to release The Clash Mark II's only single, 'This Is England', presumably on the reasonable grounds that it wasn't.

ALBUMS

The Clash had an unusual attitude to albums, partly because of their CBS deal. Keen to release as many sides as possible, in the ill-fated belief (didn't they have lawyers?) that it would free them from their contract, they also gave in to commercial pressures on two significant records, *Give 'Em Enough Rope* and *Combat Rock*, with excellent chart results but poor artistic ones. All Clash albums, however, are worthy of investigation. Two – the UK version of *The Clash* and *London Calling* – are essential.

The Clash (UK version)

Released: April 1977
Chart position: UK: 12
Producer: Mickey Foote

Janie Jones/Remote Control/I'm So Bored With The
USA/White Riot/Hate And War/What's My Name?/
Deny/London's Burning/Career Opportunities/
Cheat/Protex Blue/Police And Thieves/48 Hours/
Garageland

*Joe Strummer's favourite and who would argue with
him? Recorded in just a few weeks, The Clash is a great
punk icon. From its brilliant sleeve – on the front, a
ripped-up picture of three of the band posing like crazy
in an alley, in the manner of The Ramones; on the back,
a shot from the Notting Hill riots, and dayglo typogra-
phy everywhere else – to its incendiary tracklisting, like
most debut albums,* The Clash *is by and large a snap-
shot of the band's then-current stage set.* The Clash
*exploded almost instantly into thousands of people's
record collections.*

*It didn't sound like a classic rock album at the time,
in the conventional meaning of the phrase. Playing is
raw and just about in tune. Singing – both· Strummer's
phlegmy roar and Jones's cawing – is incoherent and
apparently not in English. And Mickey Foote's production is tinny and compressed. By the standards of the
late 1970s, an era where smoothness, mellow grooves
and multi-tracking were the dull, dead benchmarks of a
very complacent industry, it sounds awful, but to the
people who bought it, the sound of* The Clash *was
something new and very exciting.*

*Others disagreed; one writer described the production
as 'Winfield stereo', while no lesser authority than the
always peeved Johnny Rotten (who also claimed to have
heard of reggae before* The Clash*) said the album sound-*

ed like a folk record. Which, in a good way, it was. Where The Sex Pistols' records were huge and rocky, The Clash's early work sounded fast, instant and ramshackle. From Terry Chimes's glam rock football-terrace drums on 'Janie Jones' all the way to Mick Jones's hamfisted anthemic introduction to 'Garageland', The Clash was an album packed with musical ideas all busting a gut to get out.

With all this compressed energy, it's no surprise that the album was shortweight even by punk's speedy standards, so the band decided to include a lengthy version of the then-current reggae hit, 'Police And Thieves', a highly biblically-referenced song by the sweetly-voiced Junior Murvin. Murvin's version is an almost angelic, wistful account of the evils of life that will one day be eased by Jah. The Clash's, naturally, is an apocalyptic saga of corruption and punishment with a spoken Strummer introduction that owes something to the Sex Pistols' early versions of 'Anarchy In The UK', where Rotten sneered the words 'Bible quotation number three!' and a brilliantly devised Mick Jones arrangement where he and Strummer alternate their hammering, on/off-beat guitars. In that one song, The Clash introduced a new musical fusion and brought two completely different groups – white punks and West Indians – into the same arena. After that, racism and punk were never going to mix.

The rest of the record is the classic punk mix of wild enthusiasm disguised as disgust and contempt. Shane MacGowan once summed up the difference between punk and 1980s music by declaring sagely that 'When we were excited, we sang about being bored. Now we are bored, we sing about being excited.' So Joe

Strummer, who loved America to death, sang 'I'm So Bored With The USA'. So 'Deny' and 'Cheat' are fantastically up songs. And best of all, there's The Clash's first underdog song, 'Garageland' which boasts about how crap they are. This was punk, despite the fact that Strummer had a background in R&B and blues and had once named himself after Bob Dylan's idol Woody Guthrie, and despite the fact that Mick Jones had once been a virtual rock guitar hero in the Keith Richards mode. This was Year Zero. The Clash had formed because of The Sex Pistols, not because of any sense of rock's history, and they were going to make sure they sounded like nothing in rock's history whatsoever.

Twenty-plus years later, when debates about production, selling out and who went to what school are old history, it's possible to hear The Clash *as both a great punk album – it has songs about lying, fat old politicians and unemployment – and as a great Clash album, with all their obsessions already in place: reggae, London, America, and of course The Clash themselves.*

The Clash (US version)

Released: July 1979
Chart position: US: 100
Producer: Mickey Foote

Clash City Rockers/I'm So Bored With The USA/ Remote Control/Complete Control/White Riot/ (White Man) In Hammersmith Palais/London's Burning/I Fought The Law/Janie Jones/Career

Opportunities/What's My Name?/Hate And War/
Police And Thieves/Jail Guitar Doors/Garageland

*They'd already messed up with the singles, so Epic
America decided to make things worse by slapping a
few early British 45s – milestones like '(White Man) In
Hammersmith Palais' and 'Complete Control', neither of
which admittedly would have received airplay on late
1970s US FM radio alongside Foreigner's 'Feels Like The
First Time', onto the debut album. They moved the
group's name up to the top to aid store-browsing and
changed the sleeve colour for people who didn't like
dark colours. They gave away a free single. Oh, and they
included the single 'Clash City Rockers' at its proper,
slightly slower speed, to ensure that obsessive British
collectors bought this album too. Half premature
Greatest Hits and half debut album, the American version of* The Clash *is a mangled, bizarre thing that still
contains no bad songs. Thanks to Epic's ineptitude and
FM radio's resistance to anything that wasn't at least as
dull as The Eagles, it only reached Number 100 in the
Billboard charts. Canadians were even luckier, being
able to purchase the album in a lovely dark blue sleeve.*

Give 'Em Enough Rope

Released: November 1978
Chart position: UK: 2
US: 128
Producer: Sandy Pearlman

Safe European Home/English Civil War/
Tommy Gun/Julie's Been Working For The Drug
Squad/Last Gang In Town/Guns On The Roof/
Drug-Stabbing Time/Stay Free/Cheapskates/
All The Young Punks (New Boots And Contracts)

*Having made a huge impact on Blue Oyster Cult, pro-
ducer Sandy Pearlman was a record company-inspired
choice for the second Clash album. They hit it off, albeit
not in the conventional sense, for when he came to meet
the band before a show, Pearlman was punched in the
face by a Clash roadie. The Clash found that suddenly
they were an American band. Epic wanted them to be
successful in the USA and felt that the tinny rants of the
first album were not the way forward, which is why, con-
fusingly,* Give 'Em Enough Rope *came out before* The
Clash *in America. Bringing out Jones's rock side (some
accounts claim that 'Safe European Home' once bor-
rowed the riff to a Sammy Hagar tune), Pearlman
famously brought the guitars way upfront and put Joe
Strummer's voice miles back in the mix. While this could
easily have resulted in a superb rock record – as the first
three tracks suggest – the problem was that The Clash's
new material was a lot weaker than that on the debut.*

This time there were three songs about being The

Clash – the feeble 'Guns On The Roof' the chest-beating 'Cheapskates', and the ridiculous 'Last Gang In Town'. That leaves 'Stay Free', which is wonderful, and features Jones's best guitar solo, the muddy 'All The Young Punks (New Boots And Contracts)', and 'Julie's Been Working For The Drug Squad', a piano-roll boogie about the British anti-drug police action, Operation Julie, which is in some ways a precursor of the eclecticism of *London Calling*, and in others just plain embarrassing.

Once you get past the sleeve – a retinted souvenir postcard from Tombstone that appears to have been designed by some little boys – the record begins superbly. 'Safe European Home', about Strummer's reactions to his first trip to Jamaica, starts and ends with blistering riffs, cannoning drums and Strummeresque rants about rudies (rude boys – Jamaican bad boys). It's one of the best things The Clash ever did, from its superfast introduction, to Strummer's chant of 'Rudie come from Jamaica/Rudie can't fail' (later stolen by Clash fans Manic Street Preachers for their 'Roses In The Hospital'), a single that never was, and it even turned up in Joe Strummer's 1999 solo concert dates.

'Tommy Gun' – whose scattergun drum introduction was suggested by new recruit Topper Headon – is a wild anti-war rant with a brilliant one-note Jones solo (lifted from Glenn Campbell's 'Wichita Lineman' via David Bowie's 'Starman'). 'English Civil War' is the same thing, set to a traditional folk tune. This album is so filled with war and weapons, it could have been called *The Clash: Guns R Us*.

The Clash suffered severely in the UK for *Give 'Em*

Enough Rope, *which was seen as pandering to US tastes, being self-obsessed and the work of a band who were, in the most popular phrase of the era, selling out. Now it can be seen as the work of a band trying to come to terms with what they were, and the contradictions of being a punk act who were more than two-chord wonders. The next album would resolve all these contradictions.*

London Calling

Released: December 1979
Chart position: UK: 9
US: 27
Producer: Guy Stevens

London Calling/Brand New Cadillac/Jimmy Jazz/
Hateful/Rudie Can't Fail/Spanish Bombs/The Right
Profile/Lost In The Supermarket/Clampdown/
The Guns Of Brixton/Wrong 'Em Boyo/Death Or
Glory/Koka Kola/The Card Cheat/Lover's Rock/
Four Horsemen/I'm Not Down/Revolution Rock/
Train In Vain

'No Elvis, Beatles or The Rolling Stones!' Strummer sang on '1977'. In 1979, he recorded an album which featured songs that sounded like all three. In the middle of 1979, The Clash were floundering. They had begun to enjoy some commercial success with the release of The Cost Of Living *EP, whose astute rebel-rock cover of The Bobby Fuller Four's 'I Fought The Law' had*

received lots of airplay, while sending out a cartoony image of the naughty Clash men, and in doing so had shaken off the last lumps of punk orthodoxy. At the time British punk was re-evolving into a horrible Mohican-and-studded-jacket, wino-on-a-park-bench self-parody.

Unfortunately, their new direction was a woolly, pointless one. The Cost Of Living's 'Gates Of The West' and 'Groovy Times' were clumsy pop songs whose acoustic guitars, vague sentiments and (yet again) rants about going to America suggested that The Clash were evolving into a bad-tempered version of Wings, while the fact that 'I Fought The Law' was a cover of someone else's song and that 'Capital Radio' was a cover of their own song suggested that ideas were becoming a problem for The Clash. As the best bands of the era – Gang Of Four, Buzzcocks, The Specials – were mutilating punk thrash into new kinds of music, The Clash briefly seemed to be lurching towards the horrors of the past.

Returning to the studio, The Clash decided to work with the producer of their original 1977 demos, Guy Stevens. Stevens was an unpredictable man with both a brilliant musical reputation and a terrible personal one. Most importantly, the people he had worked with – Chuck Berry, early reggae acts, Mott The Hoople – were all legends in the Clash iconography. Amazingly, Stevens turned out to be the saviour of The Clash. His highly individual approach to producing – waving chairs about, pouring beer into pianos, hypnotising Joe Strummer into writing songs – suited their highly individual approach to rock 'n' roll. London Calling was to be the best thing either party would ever do.

Coming out to a mixture of rapture and indignation from the British music press, who either hated it for not being 'White Riot' times ten or loved it for being what it really was – The Clash's interpretation of the entire history of rock, minus the bad bits – London Calling *stood out as a supremely confident, authoritative record that even sounded great the day you first played it. With its sparse but loud production, its wild mixture of musical styles, and its immensity – nearly 20 tracks from a punk group? Blimey! –* London Calling *just stands there and says proudly, 'I am a great album.'*

Released in Britain in December 1979, in time to save record buyers from a depressing Christmas, the album came out in the USA a month later, enabling the always quick-on-the-uptake grandpas of Rolling Stone *magazine to make it their album of the 1980s (presumably* Rubber Soul *was their album of the 1990s). Even the sleeve is great – a pastiche by cartoonist Ray Lowry of Elvis Presley's first UK album, with a Pennie Smith photo of Paul Simonon trashing his bass onstage.*

Track by track, it's an almost flawless record. 'London Calling' itself, with its memorably ominous bass riff, urgent guitars and classic Apocalypse Now *Strummer vocal, which seems to concern the end of the world, the River Thames flooding, and a nuclear meltdown, and ends with a quote from 'Singing The Blues', a 1950s rock 'n' roll song covered recently by Dave Edmunds. Aptly, the next track is 'Brand New Cadillac', a cover of a song by British rock 'n' roller Vince Taylor (whose later onstage declaration that he was Christ inspired Ziggy Stardust). Strummer famously complained that The Clash's version sped up at the end. 'All great rock* records speed up,' replied Stevens.

Rock occurs on 'Hateful', 'I'm Not Down' and the superb 'Clampdown'. There's reggae on Paul Simonon's 'The Guns Of Brixton' (a tune later used as the basis for 'Dub Be Good To Me', a British number One for Beats International, an early vehicle for Fatboy Slim), ska on 'Wrong 'Em Boyo' and even soul on their breakthrough American hit 'Train In Vain', a song that was, amazingly, nearly given away free with copies of the NME, which is why it wasn't listed on the original sleeve or the trendy new millennial issue. 'Train In Vain', equally amazingly, is one of the few Clash songs covered by another artist, namely Annie Lennox, of all people, and it was sampled by Garbage for 'Stupid Girl'.

But there are new areas where London Calling takes off. Mick Jones rewrites 'I Fought The Law' as a Phil Spector ballad about a doomed loner in 'The Card Cheat', while on the almost new wave disco 'Lost In The Supermarket' he sings his most human vocal ever. 'Spanish Bombs' is virtually a Beatles song about the Spanish Civil War (with references to DC9s, a plane which was regularly crashing at the time) and was apparently Mick Jones's gran's favourite Clash song (see? No one likes 'Red Angel Dragnet'). And, oddest of all, was 'The Right Profile', a song written because Guy Stevens had just read a biography of the actor Montgomery Clift and had psyched Strummer out into writing about him.

There are low points. 'Koka Kola' is one note about nothing. 'Lover's Rock' is, scarily, Joe Strummer singing about love and sex. And The Clash's self-obsession is never funnier than on 'Death Or Glory' or 'Four Horsemen': they were a band, not a cavalry regiment, for goodness sake. But these moments are few and far between; London Calling is one of the most extraordinary albums ever. It sounds like a perfect rock record precisely because it doesn't sound like any other rock record ever made.

London Calling could be a Rolling Stones album if The Rolling Stones had had the humour and wit without the cynicism and arrogance, it could be a Beatles album if The Beatles had ever been really mad about everything, it could even be a Sex Pistols album if The Sex Pistols had been able to compress the entire history of rock, soul, punk and reggae into one short, busy hour. In the end, London Calling is a great album that only The Clash – with their disparate musical blend of Strummer's shamanistic, self-mythologising, street-preaching, reggae madman ranting, Jones's urban rock star image and alienated yowling and Simonon's love of cool gangster posing. London Calling is such a perfect blend of the best of their work, it could have been subtitled 'Everything You Wanted To Know About The Clash But Were Too Scared To Ask'.

The follow-up, inevitably, would be something of a disappointment. However, The Clash being The Clash, even the disappointments were exciting.

Sandinista!

Released: December 1980
Chart postition: UK: 19
US: 24
Producers: The Clash

The Magnificent Seven/Hitsville UK/Junco Partner/
Ivan Meets GI Joe/The Leader/Something About
England/Rebel Waltz/Look Here/The Crooked
Beat/Somebody Got Murdered/One More Time/
One More Dub/Lightning Strikes (Not Once But
Twice)/Up In Heaven (Not Only Here)/Corner
Soul/Let's Go Crazy/If Music Could Talk/The Sound
Of The Sinners/Police On My Back/Midnight Log/
The Equaliser/The Call-Up/Washington Bullets/
Broadway/Lose This Skin/Charlie Don't Surf/
Mensforth Hill/Junkie Slip/Kingston Advice/The
Street Parade/Version City/Living In Fame/Silicone
On Sapphire/Version Pardner/Career Opportunities/
Shepherds Delight

*One of the great legends about The Clash is that they
made* London Calling *a double album and* Sandinista! *a
triple because they thought that they would get out of
their CBS contract faster, and then discovered that no
matter how many discs they released with each album,
they still only counted as one record. Unlike most of the
great legends of The Clash, this one is actually true. Joe
Strummer likes to cite* Sandinista! *as an extraordinarily
daring career move, but it was an extraordinarily silly one.*

*Triple albums have an extremely bad name in rock.
From George Harrison to Crosby, Stills, Nash & Young,
the triple album has always been seen as a disc too far,
generally to be filled up with some songs that would
normally be hard pressed to get jobs as B-sides or,
worse, a live 'jam' or similar horror. Punk rock — which
set great store in brevity, and dictated that nothing
should be more than two and half minutes long — made*

things worse; there were new rules for albums. The Jam once decided to make a concept album, but scrapped it because concept albums weren't punk. And triple albums were very much not punk. After the huge dare of London Calling, The Clash were riding high. Sandinista! nearly finished them.

Its size was not the only problem. Like The Beatles' so-called White Album (another record which is overlong because the band were trying to record themselves out of their contract), Sandinista! is a record that most people always say would have been a great single album. Unlike The Beatles' so-called White Album, sadly, Sandinista! isn't exactly chock-a-block with great songs in the first place. A Clash fan's 90-minute tape of the ideal short Sandinista! would almost certainly contain the hilarious 'The Magnificent Seven' (Strummer discovers both rap and the fact that 'mobster' rhymes with 'lobster'), the brilliant cover of The Equals' 'Police On My Back' and the song that could be its companion piece, Mick Jones's 'Somebody Got Murdered' (another heroic Jones outlaw-with-a-conscience tune), Joe Strummer's wonderful, downbeat 'Broadway', with its great opening line, 'It ain't my fault it's six o'clock in the morning,' (and a song that The Clash used to open their live shows with), the Apocalypse Now tribute (like The Clash weren't going to write one of those – Apocalypse Now could almost be renamed One Night In Joe Strummer's Head) 'Charlie Don't Surf', and the jaw-droppingly good 'The Call-Up', but beyond that, there are few great songs.

The Clash were a band so desperate to cover six sides of vinyl that they resorted to filler. So we get 'Junco

Partner', a song that was part of The 101'ers' repertoire and should have stayed there, yet another 'I Fought The Law' rewrite in 'Washington Bullets' (one day some bootlegger with a cruel sense of humour will put out a CD EP of 'I Fought The Law', 'Washington Bullets', 'The Card Cheat', and 'Wrong 'Em Boyo') and lazy stuff like the vague rockabilly of 'The Leader' and the insanely dreadful 'Hitsville UK'. Oddly, the version of 'Career Opportunities', sung by keyboard player Mickey Gallagher's children Luke and Ben, is still quite charming. Twenty years later, in a bizarrely splendid moment of rock trivia, the Gallagher brothers formed the British indie group Little Mothers and went on tour supporting Joe Strummer. Very nice.

There are moments where the listener wishes more time had been spent on material. 'The Sound Of The Sinners' sees mad preacher Strummer actually turn into a real preacher. 'Ivan Meets GI Joe' could have been a lot more than vocalist Topper Headon's first try-out for 'Rock The Casbah'. And Mick Jones seems to have written a grand total of one song, 'Somebody Got Murdered'. Sandinista! appears to be very much Joe Strummer's album. It certainly isn't Paul Simonon's — he doesn't even play on some of the more dancey tracks like 'The Magnificent Seven', his part being taken by Norman Watt-Roy, who, like Mickey Gallagher, was one of Ian Dury & The Blockheads (and later went on to play even more clandestine bass on Frankie Goes To Hollywood's 'Relax').

Sandinista!'s mad length is partly redeemed by Mikey Dread's immensely likeable, but hardly essential (unless one is a committed dopehead) dub side, which is The

Clash in the chill-out room and serves to throw Sandinista!'s enormous obsession with the USA into sharp relief. The very Andrew Cronshaw swirl of 'Rebel Waltz' is a fine tune but does beg the question of how many armies Joe Strummer thought he was in.

In the end, Sandinista!'s immense length and too-often low quality did little for The Clash's credibility and sales figures, singles like 'The Call-Up' and 'The Magnificent Seven' floundered, and The Clash, being virtually based in New York, began to lose fans in their British home base, where people resented their desire to be in the USA, of which once they had been famously bored. Alas, The Clash found that, while they loved America, America did not love them back. Yet.

Combat Rock

Released: May 1982
Chart position: UK: 2
US: 7
Producer: Glyn Johns

Know Your Rights/Car Jamming/Should I Stay Or Should I Go?/Rock The Casbah/Red Angel Dragnet/Straight To Hell/Overpowered By Funk/Atom Tan/Sean Flynn/Ghetto Defendant/Inoculated City/Death Is A Star

As The Clash's career began to unravel and they actually spent a year (1981) without releasing an album, the group decided to make a record that would be in

many ways the opposite of its recent predecessors. For the first time in four years, the band would make a single album, instead of a double or a triple; they would hire an outside producer, rather than do it themselves; and they would make it look modern and marketable, rather than Xeroxed and instant. From the colour cover shot – the band photographed in novelty combat fatigues by Pennie Smith on a railroad track in Thailand – to the choice of producer and arranger Glyn Johns, who'd begun his career as an engineer on The Beatles' so-called White Album, Combat Rock *was the most professional piece of work The Clash had recorded. And this diligence paid off; aided by constant touring,* Combat Rock *went to Number 7 in the American charts and made them proper stars for the first time in their career.*

Being The Clash, of course, it sounded like nothing else in the charts. It was eclectic – punk sat next to rap, Rolling Stones rock 'n' roll stared happily at rock disco, and everyone, from Tymon Dogg, idiotic graffiti artist Futura 2000, and former support act Joe Ely to Allen Ginsberg turned up to add an extra dimension. The band's crony and sometime manager Kosmo Vinyl is even on one track, the appalling 'Red Angel Dragnet', for reasons none can fathom. There is no reggae present, but this apart, The Clash's musical experimentalism, this time tied strongly to their full-time presence in New York City, is very much in effect.

On paper, Combat Rock *sounded admirable. Lyrics dealt variously with civil rights, Vietnam and the decline of empire, girlfriend problems and the state of Iran. There was even a Robert De Niro impression. However, on vinyl, things were not so good. Musically,* Combat Rock *is a couple of superb tracks resting in a thick grim gravy of dullness. Topper Headon's heroin problem was in full swing, and perhaps this accounts for the record's lacklustre feel, or maybe Glyn Johns's slick and efficient production numbed the sound with a record store-friendly wall of wool. Certainly there are too many songs here that just sound like vague, toothless jam sessions; even the funk track 'Overpowered By Funk' sounds like it should have been called 'Overpowered By Dullness'. Conversely, 'Rock The Casbah' is a tune so chirpy that Will Smith sampled it and Joe Strummer named his label after it.*

The Clash were very much in love with New York but it was a musical inspiration that somehow didn't suit them; even an exultant song like 'Car Jamming', despite its sense of delight, ultimately boils down to a fairly pointless song about listening to music in a traffic jam: exciting to be there, but not deeply thrilling to the listener, who may wish to compare the spooky, jet-lagged ambience of a non-album song like 'First Night Back In London', which was recorded around the same time. Cool and exciting The Clash certainly were, but they were not a band from New York, a city whose sense of cool often revolves around irony rather than the enthusiasm The Clash always had in abundance.

The album is too full of New York, but The Clash, like an excited tourist just back from vacation, had little else to talk about, and they filled Combat Rock *with the city's people, real or imagined. And as Allen Ginsberg mumbled bad poetry about dances (names of dances supplied by Joe Strummer, who could have written*

Ginsberg's part in his sleep), *as Kosmo Vinyl shouted like a fool, as Futura 2000 painstakingly wrote out a graffiti lyric sheet, The Clash were falling apart. Strummer and Simonon were barely talking to Jones, and the songs suffered massively as a result. No one seems to give a damn – even the cover shot looks like four people pretending to be The Clash – and it would soon all be over. Several of the song titles – 'Death Is A Star', 'Straight To Hell', 'Inoculated City' – indicated the same thing.*

This is not to say, however, that Combat Rock *is a worthless record. Thanks to Strummer's wit and ever-active mind and his enormous heart, there are one or two redeeming moments. 'Know Your Rights' is a half-return to the shouty punk glory days, all rockabilly and vague political anger; it's never quite clear who Strummer is having a go at, but he comes over caustically enough to scare anyone.*

Mick Jones's 'Should I Stay Or Should I Go?' is a funny song, with counter-lyrics sung in – fact – Ecuadorian Spanish translated by engineer Eddie Garcia's mother. And there is a certain irony in the title of the last single written by Mick Jones before Strummer and Simonon sacked him. 'Rock The Casbah' has a splendid piano riff (written by Topper Headon) and a droll Strummer lyric. And the album's best song is also a great Clash moment. 'Straight To Hell', with its rough bossa nova beat and fantastic chiming guitar, is a powerful journey of a lyric and an astonishing vocal performance from Strummer, a song about the bastard child of a Vietnamese mother and an American GI, about King Solomon's justice, and about the end of the British Empire. Bleak and at the same time compassionate,

'Straight To Hell' was a song that took all The Clash's fantasies — war, Vietnam, England, sloganeering — and for once made them into something moving and epically sad. When Strummer sings, 'Let me tell you about your blood, bamboo kid/ It ain't Coca-Cola, it's rice', for the first and only time on a Clash song about war, imperialism and injustice, he doesn't sound excited and angry, he sounds weary and resigned, the truth too heavy to carry.

After this record was released, half the band departed, first Headon (replaced by the uncomplaining Terry Chimes) and then Jones, to be replaced by a lot of people. The Clash was all over bar the shouting, but there was a lot of shouting to come.

Cut The Crap

Released: November 1985
Chart position: UK: 16
            US: 85
Producers: Joe Strummer, José Unidos, Bernie Rhodes

Dictator/Dirty Punk/We Are The Clash/Are You Red…Y/Cool Under Heat/Movers And Shakers/ This Is England/Three Card Trick/Play To Win/ Fingerpoppin'/North And South/Life Is Wild

They were known as The Clash Mark II, a name which suggested some equality between the two versions of the group, but, whatever the merits of this underrated album, The Clash Mark II were not The Clash. Even writ-

ing a song called 'We Are The Clash' could not make them The Clash, any more than writing a song called 'We Are The Qualified Airline Pilots' could make them able to fly 747s on commercial routes.

Recorded in Munich, Cut The Crap, whoever made it, is an extraordinary record made under extraordinary circumstances. Written by Strummer, and, apparently, Bernie Rhodes, the record was definitely produced by Strummer and Rhodes (as José Unidos) who layered every track with drum machines, sound effects and looped spoken-word tapes. Strummer and Simonon's new band (guitarists Vince White and Nick Sheppard, drummer Pete Howard), who contributed more to live performances than to the record, were present to add a kind of punk rock which, while very 1977, was more like the punk rock of fake terrace yobs Sham 69 than the more inventive punk of The Clash. Football chants, thrashing guitars and oddly unsubtle song titles suggested that Simonon and, in particular, Strummer were striving hard to remember what it was like to be an up-and-coming punk band.

'Dictator' and 'Dirty Punk', for all their energy and tunefulness, sound like songs written by a group who wanted to be The Clash. And in a way, they were. This band were best when they simply ignored the self-imposed punk rock blueprint; and so, despite Strummer's ill-advised Mohican on the sleeve, songs like 'This Is England' and the oddly-titled 'Are You Red... Y' are very good.

Cut The Crap has been removed from the Clash canon, officially left off the last batch of Clash CD reissues in Britain like an ugly illegitimate son. This – while typical of The Clash, a band who could out-Stalin Stalin

— is a shame, because it's not bad at all. Anyone who wants to buy albums because of what they sound like, rather than who they were made by, will find much fine music here, and a consistency and urgency utterly lacking from Combat Rock.

COMPILATIONS

The Clash have been served oddly by their compilations. The *Black Market* compilations collect all the non-album tracks and work best if you have all the regular albums already, while *The Story Of The Clash* and *On Broadway* both seem not quite complete somehow. Still, all are excellent and (with the exception of *On Broadway*) get cheaper every day.

Black Market Clash

1980
Capital Radio One/The Prisoner/Pressure Drop/
Cheat/City Of The Dead/Time Is Tight/Bankrobber
— Robber Dub/Armagideon Time/Justice Tonight/
Kick It Over

After three years, The Clash had many uncollected songs knocking around. Black Market Clash *— with its excellent sleeve shot and its trendy 10-inch vinyl packaging — was a sensible attempt to put a few rarities together. 'Capital Radio One' had been an NME single,*

'The Prisoner', 'Pressure Drop' and 'City Of The Dead' were early, excellent, B-sides, while 'Cheat' was one of the songs that had fallen off the American version of the first album. 'Bankrobber/Robber Dub' was the full version of the Mikey Dread collaboration, and 'Time Is Tight' is a charming, if slightly off-the-wall cover version of the Booker T & The MGs instrumental hit, made even more strange by the fact that it is a keyboard instrumental played on guitars. Best of all, however, is the inclusion of the superb 'Armagideon Time' and its two almighty dubs, laid out in a row for extra listening pleasure.

This LP was later reissued in somewhat different form as Super Black Market Clash, but is a lot more fun in this format, particularly if you want to listen to all the versions of 'Armagideon Time' together, rather than over a period of days.

The Story Of The Clash

Released: 1988

The Story Of The Clash Vol 1

Released: 1991

The Magnificent Seven/Rock The Casbah/This Is Radio Clash/Should I Stay Or Should I Go?/Straight To Hell/Armagideon Time/Clampdown/Train In Vain/The Guns Of Brixton/I Fought The Law/ Somebody Got Murdered/Lost In The Supermarket/Bankrobber/(White Man) In Hammersmith Palais/London's Burning/Janie Jones/ Tommy Gun/Complete Control/Capital Radio One/White Riot/Career Opportunities/Clash City Rockers/Safe European Home/Stay Free/London Calling/Spanish Bombs/English Civil War/ Police And Thieves

This record is a suitable starting point for the juvenile Clash fan, being the only consistent compilation that doesn't cost a small fortune. Originally released in 1988 as a double album merely titled The Story Of The Clash, The Story Of The Clash Vol. 1 *(we still do not anticipate a second volume unless CBS are really going to make* The Clash *record the rest of those eight contracted albums) is, so far, the only properly thought-out collection of Clash music.* On Broadway *doesn't count, as it's not so much a compilation, more a complete back catalogue with bits missing. Released by the ever-*

vigilant CBS with a backwards track listing which cleverly creates the impression that The Clash began their career as an odd dance group and gradually became an aggressive punk group, The Story of The Clash is a fine collection which also manages to suggest that someone at the record company really doesn't like the first Clash album.

There are no surprises on this record; most favourites are here, and there is even the NME version of 'Capital Radio', with an interview where Strummer and Jones try to out-Cockney interviewer Tony Parsons. Joe Strummer also contributes mythomaniac sleevenotes in the persona of fictional Clash valet Albert Transom which are, to say the least, not deeply informative, but do contain several entertaining anecdotes that are, in classic Strummer style, true on an emotional level rather than a factual one.

Crucial Music: The Clash Collection

Released: 1989

Clash City Rockers/Police And Thieves/Tommy Gun/Stay Free/Safe European Home/Train In Vain/ Clampdown/The Magnificent Seven/Police On My Back/Straight To Hell

A cheapo American compilation which, apparently, manages to miss a few seconds off the start of 'Clash City Rockers'. Weren't CBS just the best?

Crucial Music: The Clash – 1977 Revisited

Released: 1990

1977/London's Burning (Live)/Deny/Cheat/
48 Hours/Protex Blue/Groovy Times/Gates Of The
West/1–2 Crush On You/Stop The World

*A total mess of a compilation, designed to complement
the US version of* The Clash *with a selection of duff
Clash songs.*

The Singles Collection

Released: 1991

White Riot/Remote Control/Complete Control/
Clash City Rockers/(White Man) In Hammersmith
Palais/Tommy Gun/English Civil War/I Fought The
Law/London Calling/Train In Vain/Bankrobber/
The Call Up/Hitsville UK/The Magnificent
Seven/This Is Radio Clash/Know Your Rights/Rock
The Casbah/ Should I Stay Or Should I Go?

*Released on the back of a Levi's advertisement, this
compilation is short and oddly pointless (for a great singles band, an awful lot of the Clash's best material is
only available on albums – especially if you're a happy
customer of Epic Records of America) but does enable
'Hitsville UK' to be owned by people who don't want it
(i.e. nearly everyone). Pedants may note that, despite*

*their double-A-side nature, several singles are repre-
sented only by their hit sides. 'Straight To Hell' is omitted
in favour of 'Should I Stay Or Should I Go?', 'Armagideon
Time' left out in favour of 'London Calling' and 'Groovy
Times', 'Gates Of The West' and 'Capital Radio Two' are
missing in favour of 'I Fought The Law'.*

*This CD was only released in the UK. An American
Clash singles compilation would be about 10 minutes
long and have 'Should I Stay Or Should I Go' on it six
times.*

On Broadway

Released: 1994

Janie Jones (demo)/Career Opportunities (demo)/
White Riot/1977/I'm So Bored With The USA/
Hate And War/What's My Name/Deny/London's
Burning/Protex Blue/Police And Thieves/48 Hours/
Cheat/Garageland/Capital Radio One/Complete
Control/Clash City Rockers/City Of The Dead/
Jail Guitar Doors/The Prisoner/Pressure Drop/1–2
Crush On You/English Civil War (live)/I Fought The
Law (live)/Safe European Home/Tommy Gun/Julie's
Been Working For The Drug Squad/Stay Free/One
Emotion/Groovy Times/Gates Of The West/
Armagideon Time/London Calling/Brand New
Cadillac/Rudie Can't Fail/The Guns Of Brixton/
Spanish Bombs/Lost In The Supermarket/The Right
Profile/The Card Cheat/Death Or Glory/
Clampdown/Train In Vain/Bankrobber/Police On My

Back/The Magnificent Seven/ The Leader/The Call-Up/Somebody Got Murdered/Washington Bullets/ Broadway/Lightning Strikes (Not Once But Twice) (live)/Every Little Bit Hurts/Stop The World/ Midnight To Stevens/This Is Radio Clash/Cool Confusion/Red Angel Dragnet/Ghetto Defendant/ Rock The Casbah/Should I Stay Or Should I Go?/ Straight To Hell/Street Parade

The 3-CD box set, but done in typically Clash-like slap-dash style. More demos, more live material, no 'Capital Radio Two', too much Combat Rock, *but one fine unre-leased track, a duet between Jones and Chrissie Hynde on the soul classic 'Every Little Bit Hurts', and one superb one (which Strummer doesn't even remember recording), the moving 'Midnight To Stevens', a beautiful paean to Guy Stevens and probably one of the few heartfelt tributes to a producer ever recorded. The book-let inside, put together by Kosmo Vinyl, is a slab of Clash mythology with several entertaining stories, while the lyric booklet demonstrates, in a good way, just how sur-real a lot of Joe Strummer's lyrics were compared to other punk songs. The* Sandinista! *selection is good, but completely ignores the excellent dub tracks; and does the world need another version of 'Lightning Strikes (Not Once But Twice)'? It does not. Two other live tracks are taken from 'Rude Boy' and demo tracks from the Guy Stevens sessions; more in both these veins was to follow, fortunately. A fairly complete, but strangely uneven and lumpy collection.*

Twelve Inch Mixes

Released: 1992

London Calling/The Magnificent Dance/This Is
Radio Clash/Rock The Casbah/This Is England/
Last Dance

The Clash were not known for their remixes, and this is yet another
deeply inessential compilation which hopefully has by now withered
and died. It did, however, acknowledge, 'This Is England'.

Super Black Market Clash

Released: 1993

1977/Listen/Jail Guitar Doors/The City Of The
Dead/The Prisoner/Pressure Drop/1–2 Crush On
You/Groovy Times/Gates Of The West/Capital
Radio Two/Time Is Tight/Justice Tonight/Kick It
Over/Robber Dub/The Cool Out/Stop The
World/The Magnificent Dance/This Is Radio Clash/
First Night Back In London/Long Time Jerk/Cool
Confusion/Mustapha Dance

The updated and less good version of Black Market
Clash *which sacrifices quality for quantity; so you get
bundles of later B-sides which aren't very good,
the dubs of 'Armagideon Time' without the original
track, which is vexing, and 'Capital Radio Two', which is
fair enough. A strange and varied compilation which*

presents a picture of The Clash going from great to much less great.

From Here To Eternity

Released: 1999

Complete Control/London's Burning/What's My Name/Clash City Rockers/ Career Opportunities/ (White Man) In Hammersmith Palais/Capital Radio/ City Of The Dead/I Fought The Law/London Calling/ Armagideon Time/Train In Vain/The Guns Of Brixton/The Magnificent Seven/Know Your Rights/ Should I Stay Or Should I Go?/Straight To Hell

Released to slavering reviews, this non-chronological live album captures The Clash at their shuddering best, Strummer ranting wildly, Jones riffing like a baboon and the rest of the band playing insanely. Containing music recorded for the film Rude Boy *and therefore almost certainly overdubbed,* From Here To Eternity *is an excellent record of a great live band at their best. If only it had been released in the era it was recorded in.*

The Clash Story

Released: 1978

Career Opportunities/White Riot/Janie Jones/ London's Burning/1977/Listen/1–2 Crush On You

A strange release, being an Italian/English biography of The Clash with lots of interesting translation errors, but largely notable for its legal inclusion of a CD of Clash demos from the Guy Stevens sessions, with Strummer's proper pronunciation of the 't's in 'White Riot'. It also includes 'Listen' from the NME EP – with Tony Parsons's interview – and what appears to be the normal version of '1–2 Crush On You'.

SINGLES

Punk rock was one of the great eras for the 7-inch single, both as a reaction against the album-oriented rock of the 1970s – bands like Pink Floyd and Led Zeppelin deeming it beneath them to release 45s – and as a cheap, fast way of releasing often topical music. The Clash, as a great punk band, were also a great singles band.

White Riot/1977

Released: April 1977
Chart position: UK: 38

From its tinny police-car bell to its insane chorus (heard by more than one early punk fan as WA WA! I WANNA WA! WA WA! WA WA WA!), 'White Riot' is one of rock history's great debut singles. Strummer wrote the lyric after he and Simonon walked around the Notting Hill

The Only Band That Matters

Left and above: Strummer and Jones in Clash-trademark poses.

Below: Live on stage c. 1977. A proto-shambolic Shane MacGowan can be seen pogoing in the bottom right hand corner.

The torturous routine of recording, c. 1979, showed both on the faces of the band and the muddy mess that was *Give 'Em Enough Rope*.

Left: The 'in no way strange' Lee 'Scratch' Perry. A huge influence on the Clash, he is famous for allegedly burning down his own studio to kill the ghosts within.

Right: Another influence on and friend of the Clash, Mikey Dread supported the band in 1979, leading to a plethora of bottle-aimed-at-opening-act incidents.

Above: Backstage on their first US tour, The Clash had yet to weary of each other and the road.
Below: Live at the Rock Against Racism festival in London's Hyde Park.

Above: The Clash Mark II sang 'We are the Clash!' They patently were not.
Below: Big Audio Dynamite, formed by Mick Jones with long-time friend Don Letts, shone brightly and briefly in the 1980s. They still tour and record regularly today.

The Clash in full 'we can play stadiums' mode. What they always wanted to become, and what their fans always feared they would become.

Above: a 47-year-old Strummer during the triumphant stage shows to promote his comeback album *Rock Art And The X-Ray Style*.
Below: Strummer, Jones and Simonon at the premiere of TV hagiography *From Westway to the World*.

Carnival, an event that year troubled by violence between police and the local black population. Strummer's rather basic philosophy was that when black people have a problem they 'don't mind throwing a brick' whereas white people, in contrast, go to school 'where they teach you how to be thick'. His naivety – which caused right-wing groups to see the song as a pro-racism song and was later faced and acknowledged on '(White Man) In Hammersmith Palais' – lent force to possibly the first record on a major label to suggest that people, white or otherwise, solve their problems by violent means.

At the time, B-side '1977', with its chorus 'No Elvis, Beatles or The Rolling Stones', was a classic statement of punk's Year Zero philosophy, but less than a year later, the song was to be something of an albatross around The Clash's neck as the band broadened their musical horizons to include a wider vision of musical history.

Remote Control /London's Burning (live)

Released: May 1977
Chart Position: UK: –

'They said 'Release 'Remote Control/We didn't want it on the label,' The Clash would sing on 'Complete Control', summing up the problem of major-label politics in one line. CBS were keen for a chart single. Insanely, legend has it, CBS chose the slowish-paced, reasonably long 'Remote Control', not so much for its football terrace chant rhythms and keening harmonies as for the fact

that it was the normal length for a single. The Clash were sticking to a central punk philosophy; no singles from albums (the British LP version of 'White Riot' is a politically acceptable, minutely different, version). The result was inevitable: the record company won. Unusually, The Clash were right; 'Remote Control' was not a big hit (and as a consequence, its 'live' – or probably just differently mixed – B-side is a collector's dream rarity). The debacle did, however, inspire one of the best singles of the era.

Capital Radio/Listen

Given away via special tokens with the British rock weekly New Musical Express, 'Capital Radio' was a slight but punchy tune about London's commercial radio station, whose bland diet of chart pop was seen by the band as unacceptable (it remains one of the few stations that if it were a person would be punched in the face for being annoying). Doctor Goebbels is mentioned, which seems a bit harsh for a station whose chief director was Richard 'Ghandi' Attenborough. The song was accompanied by an interview with NME journalist Tony Parsons, conducted on a London Underground train, in which the band talk in hilarious Cockney accents. 'Capital Radio' was later re-recorded for the Cost Of Living EP and became the inspiration for Northern Irish punk band Stiff Little Fingers' 'You Can't Say Crap On The Radio'.

Complete Control/The City Of The Dead

Released: October 1977
Chart position: UK: 28

*Having found themselves the victims of record compa-
ny shenanigans, The Clash were angry enough to go out
and record the greatest answer record of all time: a single that responded to their own 'Remote Control', bettered it and every previous Clash release, and acted as
a brilliant, enraged and inspiring commentary on
events. 'Complete Control' was the world's loudest
three-minute editorial and it still sounds exhilarating 20
years later.*

*Part of the reason for this is that, possibly stung by
criticisms of the way the first album sounded, The Clash
decided to record with one of their musical heroes, the
Jamaican reggae and dub producer Lee 'Scratch' Perry,
who had expanded the boundaries of his native music
in ways that owed very little to ska and bluebeat and
a lot to a cosmic imagination. Perry – a man who once
burned down his own studios to exorcise them of ghosts
– undoubtedly made an impression on The Clash.
However it's doubtful that they made an impression on
him, as to this day he insists that he produced not The
Clash but The Sex Pistols, although when he reported
the meeting to Bob Marley, the conversation inspired
Marley's 'Punky Reggae Party'.*

*The sonic result of this meeting is open to debate;
certainly the middle section, full of phased guitars, echo
and Strummer's rants of 'I don't trust you/Do you trust
me? HEUGGHHH!' and 'You're my guitar hero!' owes*

much to Perry's dub roots, and there is more bass than on any other Clash record so far, but the guitar-frenzied opening and sped-up fury are certainly down to engineer Bill Price (not, admittedly, qualities he displayed whilst engineering Linda McCartney's 'Seaside Woman'). Whatever its origins, 'Complete Control' is a mad, extraordinary single. Jones charges through a lyric that goes from specific gripes about the record to a more uneasy feel – 'They said we'd be artistically free/When we signed a bit of paper' and then Strummer comes in as a sarcastically preaching rocker who manages to simultaneously send up the idea of rock and prove just how powerful it can be. Jones throws off one of his Starman guitar breaks and suddenly the record crashes into a huge wall. Oddly, Epic did not release this single either, preferring to bury it on the US version of the first Clash album, where it sits tidily next to 'Remote Control').

'The City Of The Dead' is a tight song with lots of 'ooh ooh's' on it which seems to be about nothing at all very much.

Clash City Rockers/Jail Guitar Doors

Released: March 1978
Chart Position: UK: 35

While The Clash were out of the country, producer Mickey Foote took it upon himself to speed up the backing track on this slight single, possibly to make it sound more punky, possibly to draw attention away from the fact that it had the same riff as The Who's 'I Can't Explain', and possibly so no one would hear how muddy it all was. Strummer came home, heard the results, and sacked Foote, thereby ensuring The Clash might one day not sound like some men drowning in molten toffee. Meanwhile the original, slower version of the song can be found in that toilet of early Clash, the first American album.

It's a shame that 'Clash City Rockers' sounds so bad as it's a song notable for many things: the first appearance of The Clash's enormous self-obsession; the excellent 'London Calling'-like backwards guitar at the end and the fact that it's one of the few singles ever to start with the word 'and'. The title is a pun on Bay City Rollers and the reggae term 'rockers', and hearkens to Jones's beloved Mott The Hoople's habit of naming songs after themselves and writing about themselves. 'Clash City Rockers'' finest moment, apart from the guitar and voice chant at the end, is its brilliant middle eight, a parody of the London nursery rhyme 'Oranges And Lemons' which namechecks David Bowie, Gary Glitter and Jamaican DJ Prince Far I. A British jig and reel indeed.

The B-side, a 101'ers tune with new words by a very Stonesy Jonesy, is one of the best early Clash flips, with top drum noises, a rock 'n' roll riff and a chorus with the words 'Clang! Clang!' in it.

(White Man) In Hammersmith Palais/The Prisoner

Released: June 1978
Chart position: UK: 32

A huge reggae fan, Joe Strummer went to the popular

West London dance venue, Hammersmith Palais, to attend a reggae concert, an event normally attended purely by black people, mostly of West Indian extraction. He found the experience intimidating, being the only white person there and attracting more than a few looks, some of them a little pointed, but this did not surprise him. What did was the fact that the music being played and the bands performing were not his beloved roots reggae, but light Jamaican pop that bore as much resemblance to roots music as Britney Spears does to James Brown. The DJs, meanwhile, instead of playing heavy dub platters, were entertaining the crowd with Four Tops records. Strummer, slightly scared, very interested, and probably trying to score some dope, stayed, and, more importantly, mentally noted his impressions.

The result of the evening was one of the most extraordinary lyrics in pop, which begin by addressing Strummer's romantic view of how black people are, moves on to criticise other groups for their lack of idealism, and then hones back on himself, the 'all-night drug-prowling wolf who looks so sick inside'. It's a Maoist self-criticism of Strummer's attitudes and prejudices, an attack on the 'new groups', a preview of Thatcherism and a year-end diary for the new punk rock. And all this over a loose, part-reggae, part-rock backdrop with huge guitars, phased harmonica and an epic build-up which manages to work in a reference to Hitler and make it fit.

The B-side is a kitchen sink rocker about a commuter who is trapped by his own life and, were it not for Jones's speedy guitars and hysterical vocal, would have sounded like an overwrought Kinks outtake.

Tommy Gun/1–2 Crush On You

Released: December 1978
Chart Position: UK: 19
US: –

Topper Headon is famous for having two brilliant ideas (taking up heroin use was not one of them). He came up with the piano part on 'Rock The Casbah', at the time the most commercial song The Clash had record-ed, and he suggested the machine-gun rat-a-tat drum introduction to 'Tommy Gun', which is of course both thematically appropriate and musically exciting. Headon plays the introduction, the rest of the band responds loudly and things go on from there. Ostensibly about the life of a mercenary, 'Tommy Gun' is yet anoth-er song about how exciting weapons are, and features Mick Jones's best use yet of the 'Starman'/'Wichita Lineman' dada-dada-da Morse code guitar break. The Sandy Pearlman production makes this one of the loud-est Clash singles ever released, and the end features a mighty list of thrilling military words.

The B-side, conversely, is not hugely memorable, per-haps because it is a leftover Delinquents tune whose dubious lyrics about desiring schoolgirls sounded hugely dated in punk rock 1978.

English Civil War/Pressure Drop

Released: March 1979
Chart Position: UK: 25

While British DJs played this next to 'The Runaway Train Went Over The Hill' and sneered (its folk melody is also shared by the punk classic 'Nellie The Elephant', who packed her trunk and said goodbye to the circus), others noted that The Clash's obsession with military things seemed to be getting a bit out of hand lately, and this was four years before Combat Rock*. However, war was very punk rock — even Elvis Costello was to get in on this one — and violence-hating (yet somehow also violence-loving) punk rock fans did not care, preferring to dwell on 'English Civil War''s rock 'n' roll introduction, speeding-up chorus and charming Animal Farm sleeve.*

Not one of the most essential Clash A-sides — they should have put out 'Safe European Home' with 'Stay Free' on the B-side and then burned the master tapes of Give 'Em Enough Rope *— 'English Civil War' is, however, an utterly essential Clash single, featuring as it does on the B-side one of the greatest Clash cover versions ever, a rumbustious clomp through Toots & The Maytals' reggae classic 'Pressure Drop'. The Clash keep the original's ska beat but speed it up madly, add a wonderful whining Mick Jones guitar, drop the backing out halfway through and prove yet again that they could do new things to already fine songs.*

Bizarrely, Guns 'N' Roses guitarist Izzy Stradlin, of all people, did a version of The Clash's version (if you see what I mean) of 'Pressure Drop' on his debut solo album, while Robert Palmer and Johnny Depp's band P did bloody awful ones.

The Cost Of Living EP

(I Fought The Law/Capital Radio/Groovy Times/
Gates Of The West)

Released: May 1979
Chart Position: UK: 22

*Away from the public eye for several months, The Clash
found themselves isolated from the new, more experi-
mental groups and were viewed critically, with a more
cynical eye, after* Give 'Em Enough Rope. *This expensive EP was something of a holding operation, with its
remake of 'Capital Radio' (which is pretty good and
adds a sheen and bounce to a song which, while pithi-
er in its original version, was always just a little bit tinny),
its American West Coast rock tunes – the cynical
'Groovy Times' and the ooh-ooh-America-calling excite-
ment of 'Gates Of The West' – and its touchstone
moment, The Clash's cover of covers, 'I Fought The Law',
one of the few songs written by other people (this being
originally done by The Bobby Fuller Four, whose singer
was murdered by having petrol poured down his throat,
by the way). It sounds like it could have actually been a
Clash song, with its brash chorus, lines about guns, and
romantic defeatist theme.*

I Fought The Law /
(White Man) In Hammersmith Palais

Released: July 1979

Chart Position: US: –

> *Going mad, Epic actually released this single in America. With the speed of mould, they released '(White Man) In Hammersmith Palais' a year late and on a B-side, but clearly deemed The Clash's version of someone else's song an acceptable release. Which, of course, it was, even if the better song was on the B-side.*

London Calling/Armagideon Time

Released: December 1979
Chart Position: UK: 11

> *One of the greatest singles of all time, from its Ray Lowry 1950s parody sleeve to its revolutionary coupling of the album title track with a brilliant remake of the Willie Williams reggae classic 'Armagideon Time', the best Clash cover of a reggae tune (with superb dubs on the 12-inch version) whose theme – Armageddon and judgement – perfectly matched 'London Calling''s apocalyptic air. Now The Clash had moved on from punk and were inventing a new music of their own, a kind of rock which owed little to punk's mighty thrash and plenty to The Clash's other influences, reggae, soul, rockabilly, and Americana in general. Strummer's lyric is urgent, exciting and to some extent meaningless, but at the same time one of the best ever, and a song that he would continue to sing in the 1990s, both when he was singing with Shane MacGowan's Pogues and as part of his solo repertoire.*

Train In Vain (Stand By Me)/London Calling

Released: February 1980
Chart Position: US: 27

An American hit at last, ironically with the throwaway track from London Calling*. Note additional brackets on the title so the Americans weren't confused.*

Bankrobber/Rockers Galore...UK Tour

Released: August 1980
Chart Position: UK: 12

Daddy, in Joe Strummer's case, was a diplomat of course, but this song was based on some claim of Jones's that his father was in some way tangentially involved in some bank robbery, so the lyric has some basis in fact – by Clash standards, anyway. Epic famously refused to release 'Bankrobber', not because, as you might suppose, it was by The Clash, but because an executive said it sounded 'like David Bowie backwards'. It doesn't (not even 'Sound and Vision' backwards), but what it does sound similar to is 'I Fought The Law' played very slowly in a reggae style. As such, it's not the greatest of Clash reggae tunes – it's not half as good as Simonon's similarly daft 'The Guns Of Brixton' – but it has a great sound, a classic Strummer lyrical moment (the old man in the bar telling his story is a very Strummer trick), and an excellent dub B-side by Clash mate and toaster (as in Jamaican-style rapper, not bread-heating device) Mikey Dread. He was touring with The Clash regularly at this point and so knocked off a song about it.

The Call-Up/Stop The World (UK)

Released: December 1980
Chart Position: UK: 40

The Call-Up/The Magnificent Seven (US)

Released: March 1981
Chart Position: US: –

One of the best Clash singles, 'The Call-Up' was like nothing the band had recorded before, with its drum machine introduction, hypnotic beat and oddly beautiful lyric. Only Joe Strummer could write an anti-war song from the Soviet and the American perspective at the same time (there is no call-up in England), while including brilliant lines about the wheatfields of Kiev. A huge, wistful song which earns The Clash the right to call themselves a truly international band, with a wider musical palette than nearly all of their contemporaries. It should have been Number One everywhere, but instead it did badly. The B-side is a jaunty, duff tune and, a few months later, was replaced by 'The Magnificent Seven' in America.

Hitsville UK/Radio One (UK)

Released: January 1981
Chart Position: UK: 56

Hitsville UK/Police On My Back

Released: February 1981
Chart Position: US: –

This may be the worst Clash single. With lyrics apparently by Strummer, a stupid tinkling melody by Jones that was a cousin of John Fred & The Playboy Band's 1968 novelty tune 'Judy In Disguise (With Glasses)', 'Hitsville UK' is a patronising tribute to the British independent record scene, a development which had nothing whatsoever to do with The Clash and which had taken the DIY spirit of punk literally and was pumping new bands and music out on a daily basis, much to the annoyance of the major labels before they cottoned on to the idea of using them as unpaid A&R departments. Sadly for The Clash, they had signed to a major label, and were reaping the grim rewards. 'Hitsville UK' also features backing vocals by Mick Jones's girlfriend of the time, Ellen Foley, who musically had fallen very far indeed since singing on Meat Loaf's Bat Out Of Hell, *an album which effortlessly achieved the Great American Record feel that The Clash seemed so often to be striving for. Here Foley – who would later be dropped to even lower depths by Strummer and Jones on her bizarre* Spirit Of St. Louis *album – is an inaptly American voice on a song recorded by a strung-out New York rock star band. As Jones and a presumably baffled Foley namecheck labels like Small Wonder and Fast, whose heyday was passing rapidly, the listener looks at the label on the single – Epic – and wonders just how far off the point a record can be. The B-side is not memorable.*

Epic America, now getting the hang of releasing Clash singles, decided that this would be a goodie. How wrong they were; but at least it has an excellent B-side: a Jones speed-up of The Equals' 'Police On My Back', written by a young Eddy Grant, himself soon to do well with solo singles like 'I Don't Want To Dance' and 'Electric Avenue'.

The Magnificent Seven /The Magnificent Dance

Released: April 1981
Chart Position: UK: 34

Remixed from Sandinista!, *and not to its detriment, 'The Magnificent Seven' (its title a reference to the time many people get up in the morning, amongst other things) is the track that gives The Clash the right to say they were doing rap before any other white group, apart from Blondie, Talking Heads and so on. It's a superb single, utterly irreverent and daft, containing no social significance whatsoever and a brilliant two-line summary of the fiscal relationship between Karl Marx, the inventor of communism, and his benefactor, Friedrich Engels. The Clash rarely get kudos for their sense of humour, but this is a very witty single indeed, even if it does lose Mick Jones muttering 'Fucking long, innit?' at the end.*

The B-side, in keeping with the spirit of the times, is a pointless instrumental. The Americans, correctly speculating that rap was a British affair, didn't bother to release it.

This Is Radio Clash /Radio Clash/
Outside Broadcast/Radio Five 4

Released: November 1981
Chart Position: UK: 47
US: –

Oh dear. From its comedy introduction to its stupid lyric about – again – how great it is being The Clash, 'This Is Radio Clash' is Clash rapping at its feeblest, a fact CBS may have acknowledged when they released the single at a 'special' price in the UK. Its crimes are worsened by the inclusion of three instrumental B-sides, which are alike as twin brothers, one with a beard and one without. A dismal effort.

Know Your Rights/First Night Back In London

Released: May 1982
Chart Position: UK: 43
US: –

The Clash, having been away again, returned to the fray

*with their last punk rock single, an imaginatively pro-
duced affair with an excellent spoken-word rant from
Strummer. Sadly, the rest of 'Know Your Rights' is monotonous and there seems to be a lot of shouting about
not very much. The Clash, as with many bands before
them, were attempting to regain the vigour of their
youth by revisiting the music they had made in the past.
Alas, as with most bands, they were finding the results
lacking. 'Know Your Rights' is not a bad song, but it pales
hugely when set next to old Clash punk songs such as
'Complete Control', 'White Riot' or even 'Tommy Gun'.
The end was in sight.*

*Fortunately, the B-side, a song about the band going
out on their first night back home 'with the drugs in our
hair', is brilliant, an edgy, rhythmic song with an under-
tow of menace and confusion.*

Rock The Casbah/Long Time Jerk (UK)

Released: June 1982
Chart Position: UK: 30

Rock The Casbah/Inoculated City (US)

Released: October 1982
Chart Position: US: 8

*Written by Strummer and Headon (who seems, like
William Burroughs, to have become creative under the
influence of heroin), 'Rock The Casbah' is a very daft
song, based on the Ayatollah Khomeini's ban on*

Western rock music. The rest of the lyric can be explained, even if at first sight it seems to be a lot of nonsense about kings and boogie men (another reference, according to Strummer, to the bloody Clash: here is a man who took the idea 'Write about what you know' too literally). A big pop hit for the band, it also enjoyed some later success in the Gulf War when imaginative GIs discovered it could be interpreted as an attack on popular Iraqi leader Saddam Hussein.

In Britain, 'Long Time Jerk' was meandering and not much good, in the new Clash B-side tradition.

Straight To Hell/Should I Stay Or Should I Go?

Released: September 1982
Chart Position: UK: 17

CBS bravely released the fantastic, emotional and power-laden 'Straight To Hell' in the UK, only to see it sink like a stone. Its other side (it was a double-A) was marginally more popular, being an out-and-out Rolling Stones-type rocker, and showed Mick Jones in a good humour for a change. He was in the middle of what Strummer called his 'Elizabeth Taylor in a filthy mood' period at the time.

'Straight To Hell' is still one of the greatest Clash songs, but works best in an album setting, rather than on daytime radio next to Duran Duran and the evil Phil Collins. It remains in Strummer's solo act, and became the title of an Alex Cox film.

Should I Stay Or Should I Go/Cool Confusion

Released: 10 June 1982
Chart Position: US: 45

> *Epic opted for the rock, and decided that the dull 'Cool Confusion' would be a better B-side than 'Straight To Hell'...*

Should I Stay Or Should I Go?/Inoculated City

Released: 24 June 1982
Chart Position: US: –

> *...then a few months later, they changed their minds, and decided that what the public needed was another single with 'Inoculated City' on the B-side...*

Should I Stay Or Should I Go?/First Night Back In London

Released: 20 July 1982
Chart Position: US: –

> *...and then changed their minds again, put 'First Night Back In London' on the B-side, and wrapped the whole thing in a Ronald Reagan picture sleeve. It must have been very expensive being a Clash fan in America in 1982.*

This Is England/Do It Now

Released: October 1985
Chart Position: UK: 16
US: 88

By now, Jones and Headon were out and some young boys were in, and The Clash were marking their last album with this fabulous track. 'This Is England' is one of the best singles Strummer sang on, a classic lament about the state of the nation. Strummer recounts what a stranger has told him (one of Strummer's favourite lyrical devices is reporting the words of another, like the old man in the bar in 'Bankrobber', and the vagrant in 'Broadway') with a new, thrilling edge of despair.

The Clash had started their career of anger and criticism during a relatively benign, if immensely boring, Labour government. Now they found themselves with Margaret Thatcher for a Prime Minister, with a war and a crushed miners' strike behind her. Compared to Thatcher, the Queen, traditional hate focus of punk, seemed like a nice middle-aged German lady. Now England really was the oppressive country punk rock had always said it was, and now Strummer really had something to shout about. The band rise to the occasion, all monotonous riffs, clattering electronic drums and a curiously slow, droning chorus like a galley slaves' chant. A great single and, in its 12-inch form with 'Sex Mad Roar' and 'Do It Now', containing tracks better than those on Cut The Crap.

I Fought The Law/The City Of The Dead/1977/ Police On My Back/48 Hours

Released: March 1988
Chart Position: UK: 29

Pointless re-release.

London Calling/Brand New Cadillac/Rudie Can't Fail/ The Street Parade

Released: May 1988
Chart Position: UK: 46

Pointless re-release.

Return To Brixton/Return To Brixton (Extended Mix)/Return To Brixton (SW2 Dub)/ The Guns Of Brixton

Released: July 1990
Chart Position: UK: 57

The bassline from The 'Guns Of Brixton' was used by Norman Cook (later Fatboy Slim) on his single as Beats International, the hit 'Dub Be Good To Me', based on an old SOS Band tune 'Just Be Good To Me'. CBS couldn't bring out this tawdry, duff, unimaginative remix single fast enough.

Should I Stay Or Should I Go?/Rush

Released: March 1991
Chart Position: UK: 1

Thanks to the punk rock power of Levi's jeans, The Clash had a much-deserved UK Number One with this reissued single. Strummer was understandably vexed because CBS – oh, will their games never end? – put an old Big Audio Dynamite single on the B-side, thus 'Straight To Hell' never went to Number One. Later that year, the success of this single inspired opportunistic British reissues of 'Rock The Casbah' (a Number 15 after it had been the first record played on US forces radio during the Gulf War in 1990), 'London Calling' (a Number 64) and 'Train In Vain' (a big nothing), all of which are too dull to go into.

SOLO RECORDINGS

JOE STRUMMER

The 101'ers
Elgin Avenue Breakdown

Released: 1981

A collection of singles, live material and rarities from

Strummer's pub-rock band. As such, it is variable, although parts are excellent. The cover features the Metal Man, a homeless person who lived around Portobello Road and covered himself in pans and cutlery.

The 101'ers
Keys To Your Heart/5 Star Rock'n'Roll Petrol

Released: 1976

The 101er's
Sweet Revenge b/w Rabies (From The Dogs Of Love)

Released: 1981

Excellent singles from The 101'ers, although anybody who wishes to merely satisfy their curiosity slightly should buy the superb 'Keys To Your Heart', which is a fine, mad single and has a rip-roaring B-side.

Love Kills/Dum Dum Club

Released: 1986

Released as a 12-inch, from the soundtrack to the film 'Love Kills' is a catchy but anonymous rock song and is noteworthy as the only Strummer single to chart in the 1980s.

Walker: Original Motion Picture Soundtrack

Released: 1987

Filibustero/Omotepe/Sandstorm/Machete/
Viperland/Nica Libre/Latin Romance/The Unknown
Immortal/Musket Waltz/The Brooding Side Of
Madness/Tennessee Rain/Smash Everything/Tropic
Of No Returns/Tropic Of Pico

*Another Alex Cox soundtrack, this time for a film which
featured a few seconds of Strummer (he falls in a river
and has a beard). Strummer's music – a mixture of
dreamy rock and Latin – is excellent, showing that he
has a fine ear for other types of music. There are only
two songs on the record, but one, 'The Unknown
Immortals', is one of the best things he's ever recorded.*

Earthquake Weather

Released: 1989

Gangsterville/King Of the Bayou/Island Hopping/
Slant Six/Dizzy's Goatees/Shouting Street/Boogie
With Your Children/Leopardskin Limousines/
Sikorsky Parts/Jewellers And Bums/Highway One
Zero Street/Ride Your Donkey/Passport To Detroit/
Sleepwalk

*Unexceptional muddy fare, featuring an uncredited
'Latino Rockabilly War'. Its sheer ordinariness made*

Strummer chary of trying again. Epic were not especially impressed either, and the singles 'Gangsterville' and 'Island Hopping' troubled nobody.

Joe Strummer & The Mescaleros: Rock Art And The X-Ray Style

Released: 1999

Tony Adams/Sandpaper Blues/X-Ray Style/Techno D-Day/The Road To Rock 'n' Roll/Nitcomb/Diggin' The New/Forbidden City/Yalla Yalla/Willesden To Cricklewood

In 1999, Strummer returned to music full-on: touring, kicking television cameras live on stage, and releasing this excellent album, whose young band, marshalled by ex-Elastica man Antony Genn, are well up to Strummer's wide musical vision. It's a vision which encompasses reggae, rock and the nameless rhythmic music which first surfaced on 'Straight To Hell'. From the lovely 'Nitcomb' to the daft 'Tony Adams' (named after the England football captain) Rock Art And The X-Ray Style is the best thing any member of The Clash has done in years, despite a silly cover by one of Strummer's new Somerset-based friends, the artist Damien Hirst. Dedicated to 'all freedom fighters' and released in America on Hellcat, the label owned by Tim Armstrong, leader of million-selling Clash clones Rancid, it also marked the end of Strummer's association with the CBS/Columbia/Epic labels after 22 years. Turned down by most European companies until Mercury agreed to distribute it, it sold dismally and the singles 'Yalla Yalla' and 'Tony Adams' troubled nobody's charts, but time will rediscover its many charms.

MICK JONES

Mick Jones's reaction to being sacked from The Clash was to instantly form a new group – Big Audio Dynamite – with, among others, Clash film-maker Don Letts and Dan Donovan, one of Patsy Kensit's husbands. Over the years, BAD have made a lot of records, some superb, others less so. Their momentum stalled after Jones's near-fatal viral pneumonia in 1989. Try the first two and a good compilation, because, as with most groups, the quality lessens as time goes on. However, songs like 'E=MC2' and 'Medicine Show' are among the best of Jones's work.

Big Audio Dynamite:

1985: *This Is Big Audio Dynamite*
1986: *No. 10 Upping Street* (co-produced and co-written by Jones and Strummer)
1988: *Tighten Up, Vol. '88* (cover by Paul Simonon)
1989: *Megatop Phoenix*

Big Audio Dynamite II:

1990: *Kool-Aid*
1991: *The Globe*

Big Audio:

1994: *Higher Power*
1995: *F-Punk* (contains an unlisted David Bowie song)
1996: *Entering a New Ride* (unreleased)

Compilations:

1993: *The Lost Treasures Of Big Audio Dynamite I & II*
(Australia only)
1995: *Planet BAD*: Greatest Hits
1999: *Super Hits*

Mick Jones also sings on Aztec Camera's distinctly BAD-styled single 'Good Morning Britain', which reached Number 19 in the UK in 1990.

PAUL SIMONON

Paul Simonon's musical activities post-Clash have been confined to one group, Havana 3AM. Named after a jazz track and featuring the late Nigel Dixon from underrated rockabilly band Whirlwind on vocals, Havana 3AM released one eponymous LP in 1991 that no-one anywhere liked, except a few Americans who pushed it to number 169 in their chart.

TOPPER HEADON

Topper Headon released a single, 'Drumming Man', and a solo album, *Waking Up*, in 1986, recorded with guitarist Bob Tench. A eclectic big-bandy affair, tracks titled 'When You're Down', 'Just Another Hit' and 'Monkey On My Back' suggest that this album was as much creative therapy as anything else. Headon's career was effectively terminated by a prison sentence, a result of supplying heroin to a user who died.

TERRY CHIMES

Terry Chimes formed his own band, Jem, became the drummer with Bowie clones Cowboys International in the early 1980s ('Thrash' was a fantastic single) and later rejoined The Clash for a period. He also drummed with Black Sabbath and British topless model-turned-pop-singer Samantha Fox.

OTHER CLASH-RELATED PROJECTS

Elvis Costello & The Attractions
Pump It Up/Big Tears

Released: 1978

> *Mick Jones played guitar on 'Big Tears', an outtake from This Year's Model. Not good enough to make the album, but Costello did refer to it as 'my favourite outtake' from the period. Cheers, Declan.*

Various Artists
Concert For Kampouchea

Released: 1979

> *The Clash back Ian Dury on 'Sweet Gene Vincent' and '20 Flight Rock'. The reasons for this were as unclear then as they are now.*

Various Artists
RAR's Greatest Hits

Released: 1980

> *As with most major bands, The Clash have appeared on numerous compilations which need not detain us. However, this one – alongside Stiff Little Fingers, Aswad and The Mekons – did feature a brand new version of '(White Man) In Hammersmith Palais', with a severely rewritten lyric. Fantastic actually.*

Tymon Dogg
Lose This Skin

Released: 1980
> *Dogg's* Sandinista! *track, released as a single under his own name.*

Ellen Foley
The Spirit Of St. Louis

Released: 1980
> *Ellen Foley was the other vocalist on Meat Loaf's* Bat Out Of Hell *album. She also went out with Mick Jones for a time, which explains why her second solo album,* The Spirit Of St. Louis, *was written and produced by Jones and Strummer (the first was produced by Clash heroes Ian Hunter and Mick Ronson) and played on by The Clash. Anyone expecting a rocking affair in the style of her Ian Hunter-produced debut would be disappointed, however, as Jones and Strummer were going through an experimental period and wrote a lot of spooky, European ballads. A very odd album indeed.*

Ian Hunter
Short Back And Sides

Released: 1981
> *Ian Hunter's band Mott The Hoople had been a huge influence on The Clash, both in their people's rock*

stance and their self-mythologising. The Clash had even used the producer who had named the band and produced their earliest records, Guy Stevens. It is unsurprising, then, that Mick Jones took the opportunity to produce one of Hunter's solo records, Short Back & Sides. *Sadly, is not one of Hunter's best, featuring weakish songs and a not-terribly-great production. One on-line reviewer even remarked, a touch snarkily, 'I thought it was produced by Foreigner's Mick Jones.'*

Janie Jones & The Lash
House Of The Ju-Ju Queen/Sex Machine

Released: 1983

Janie Jones was the madam whose high society prostitution antics inspired the fine Clash song. Unfortunately, this single – written and performed by The Lash (Strummer, Jones, a misspelt Simonon, Blockheads Charley Charles and Mickey Gallagher, plus saxophonist Mel Collins) with Janie Jones on vocals – is less good and she's a little too old for the bondage gear on the sleeve.

Futura 2000 Featuring The Clash
Escapades Of Futura 2000/Dub

Released: 1983

Silly graffiti artist, destined to reappear on Combat Rock.

Straight To Hell
Original Soundtrack

Released: 1987

> *Strummer appears in this grim film as a greasy butler, and contributes one track, 'Ambush At Mystery Rock', under the name of Joe Strummer & The Bug Out Gang.*

Bob Dylan
Down In The Groove

Released: 1988

> *Paul Simonon, alongside ex-Sex Pistol Steve Jones, appears on 'Sally Sue Brown'. Most odd.*

The Pogues
Hell's Ditch

Released: 1990

> *Strummer has a long-standing relationship with The Pogues' then singer Shane MacGowan. As Shane Hooligan, MacGowan was a very early Clash fan and punk singer with The Nipple Erectors (later The Nips, thank God), and when MacGowan was indisposed in The Pogues, Strummer would take his place, adding 'London Calling' to the Irish folk-punks' repertoire. He also appears with the band in the ridiculous film* Straight To Hell. *But his best work with them has to be this album, an unusually relaxed affair with a sympathetic, low-key production from Strummer, who doesn't play or co-write.*

Flowered Up
A Life With Brian

Released: 1991

Flowered Up were a feisty but short-lived drug-loving North London band who employed most of The Clash's crew. Strummer contributed some of the lyrics to 'Take It' and Headon guested on percussion on 'It's On'.

The Levellers
Just The One

Released: 1995

The Levellers are a British anarchist/folk/punk group who, like Joe Strummer, are all toffs who dress down. They have had many hits in Britain and are involved in aspects of the eco-protest movement. Strummer's views are quite similar to theirs and there is a double connection. Strummer plays piano on their 'Just The One' single, returning a favour; The Levellers had done a spirited version of 'English Civil War' in 1994.

Black Grape
England's Irie

Released: 1996

Strummer befriended drug-addled 'baggy' group Black Grape and fatuous British comedian Keith Allen. The results of that friendship were some legendary anecdotes – Strummer spent an evening at the Glastonbury festival explaining to anyone who would listen that burning wood was the drugs of Henry VIII's time – and this bizarre football novelty record, which is very silly.

Brian Setzer Orchestra
Guitar Slinger

Released: 1996

> *The awful Stray Cats singer took to making big band-type records in the 1990s, with oddly renewed commercial success. Strummer's contribution here is a co-writing credit on the surfy 'Ghost Radio'. It sold millions in America.*

Various Artists
Kicks Joy Darkness

Released: 1997

> *This is a spoken-word record where everyone from Pearl Jam's Eddie Vedder to Lee Ranaldo of Sonic Youth interprets the work of overrated beat 'poet' Jack Kerouac. Strummer plays backing music to Kerouac's own reading of 'MacDougal Street Blues'.*

Grosse Pointe Blank:
Music From the Original Soundtrack

Released: 1997

More Music From The Original Soundtrack

Released: 1998

> *The first, fine soundtrack contains two old Clash tunes ('Rudie Can't Fail','Armagideon Time'). The second, inferior, volume features a new Strummer instrumental, 'War Cry', recorded with The Grid's Richard Norris.*

Various Artists
Roxy Music Tribute Album

Released: –

> *This unreleased and untitled album features a variety of acts, including ex-members of Japan and Duran Duran, performing different songs by the great Roxy Music. Strummer, not previously known for his love of arch, ironic, camp British art-rock, contributes a version of Roxy's first single, 'Virginia Plain'.*

Various Artists
Chef Aid

Released: 1998

> *No-one knows why Joe Strummer is on this very silly record; one can only suppose that either he is a huge South Park fan or he believes that Chef is a real person. His track, 'It's A Rockin' World', is however quite jaunty and not the worst song here.*

TRIBUTE ALBUMS

City Rockers: Tribute To The Clash

Released: 1999

Death Or Glory (Dave Smalley)/Clampdown (Hot Water Music)/Hate And War (Murphy's Law)/Hateful (Kid Dynamite)/Clash City Rockers (Saves The Day)/The Guns Of Brixton (Dropkick Murphys)/ Brand New Cadillac (Incognegro)/Rock The Casbah (Demonspeed)/Lost In The Supermarket (Lady Luck)/Should I Stay Or Should I Go? (Error Type 11)/Lose This Skin (Stubborn All Stars)/ London Calling (One King Down)/Train In Vain (Ill Repute)/Garageland (The Sick)/White Riot (Fang)/ Career Opportunities (Stigmata)/Straight To Hell (Skinnerbox)/Tommy Gun (The Mob)

Burning London

Released: 1999

Hateful (No Doubt)/This Is Radio Clash (Urge)/Should I Stay Or Should I Go? (Ice Cube/Mack 10/Korn)/Cheat (Rancid)/Train In Vain (Third Eye Blind)/Clampdown (Indigo Girls)/Rudie Can't Fail (The Mighty Mighty Bosstones)/(White Man) In Hammersmith Palais (311)/Lost In The Supermarket (Afghan Whigs)/White Riot (Cracker)/ London's Burning (Silverchair)/ Straight To Hell (Moby & Heather Nova)

Backlash: Tribute To The Clash

Released: 1999

Clash City Rockers (Jakkpot)/Somebody Got Murdered (Libertine)/Tommy Gun (Special Duties)/London Calling (The NC Thirteens)/The Magnificent Seven (THC)/Train In Vain (Jones Crusher)/I'm So Bored With The USA (Violent Society)/Lost In The Supermarket (Battershell)/Should I Stay Or Should I Go? (Super Green)/Police On My Back (Fang)/Complete Control (Kowalskis)/ 1977 (Electric Frankenstein)/Train In Vain (Dr. Haze & DJX-Cel)/Clampdown (Sinisters)/What's My Name? (Jones Crusher)/Rock The Casbah (The NC Thirteens)

Like an old gas fire, Clash songs should have DO NOT COVER written on them. However, a few brave fools have seen fit to have a go. The results, unsurprisingly, are universally awful. Even tribute albums to The Beatles, who wrote tunes that even a baby could sing, are generally appalling, and the power and magic of Clash songs lies as much in the performance and production as it does in the lovely tunes.

The worst of the tributes is probably *Backlash*, whose cover painting of a Union Jack-painted hammer being waved at a Mohicanned punk might give Morrissey wood but otherwise hints at a dull mixture of amateur work and Oi!-type dud punk. The best is *City Rockers*, which is equally ramshackle and full of punky unknowns (hats off to Fang, who manage to get on both albums), but has a real vigour and life to it.

Which cannot be said of the most popular compilation here, put together by The Clash's best friends in the world ever, Epic. *Burning*

London sees a lot of famous and famous-ish names blunder like fat drunks in their underwear through some awful, comprehensionless cover versions. *Burning London* makes you want to hear The Clash. But not for the reasons its compilers intended. Oh, and thank you Lord for ensuring that the rumour that Jewel was to cover 'Should I Stay Or Should I Go?' remained an unfounded one.

THREE

THE LEGACY

For a band who only made five proper albums, who never had a Number 1 in their lifetime and who split up in 1985, The Clash have had an enormous impact on people's lives. Even now, as fat bald men queue up to buy remastered CDs of *London Calling*, teenagers are buying *From Here To Eternity*, a collection of live recordings made before most of them were born. Yet, for all their critical credibility and their influence on thousands of people's lives today, The Clash did not have an easy ride when they were still with us. For every five-star review and sycophantic interview, there was a vicious critical attack on the band's ideology, credibility and shoes.

Fortunately, this sort of thing always suited The Clash. There is a piece of music by the British band Dexys Midnight Runners who were, for a while, managed by Bernie Rhodes. It is a slightly maudlin instrumental but, like most Dexys Midnight Runners songs, it has a great title; it's called 'Yes, We Must Remain The Wild-Hearted Outsiders'. As a summary of The Clash's reputation, it could hardly be bettered.

In their earliest months, from their 1976 formation to the release of the first album, The Clash were very much the wild-hearted outsiders. The rock scene was as awful and rotten as any corpse's rags. The Rolling Stones seemed to be an organisation of hideous men whose ambition was to see how many times they could meet Princess Margaret and Liza Minnelli. The Beatles had become very thirtysomething. Led Zeppelin and The Who kept forgetting to make a record every year, and would then come out with the same one they had made two years back. Bands like Genesis and Yes and Pink Floyd existed solely to keep theatrical costumiers in work and kept releasing increasingly longer albums which took longer and longer to get to the point, which generally turned out to be 'My mother wasn't nice to me', 'War is bad' or, worst of all, 'People are sheep, apart from me'.

Pop, which had been healthy during the 1970s, an era which gave birth to brilliant musical movements like glam and disco, was starting to get ill. The charts were full of revival records – rock 'n' roll and covers – and it seemed like nothing new was ever going to happen again. In this climate, it's easy to imagine that when something fresh and new like punk came along, everybody would leap at it and demand more.

In fact, the opposite was the case. Punk was deemed to be a very horrible thing indeed, except in America where it was ignored until Nirvana called it grunge. Imagine the look and music of Marilyn Manson combined with the good manners of Don King and the inner calm of Jim Carrey, dressed by vagrants and with lyrics specifically directed at you and how totally lacking in any redeeming virtues you are. And, unlike some of their contemporaries, The Clash did not fit into any popular mainstream tradition. The Stranglers were clearly

The Doors, only faster and older. The Jam were, essentially, The Who with a speech impediment. Buzzcocks wrote fast pop songs, and even The Sex Pistols, with their streamlined Chris Thomas production and the well-chosen Iggy Pop, Small Faces and Monkees cover versions and trendy Vivienne Westwood clothes, were very scary but clearly an accessible new shocking rock band.

The Clash, however, were very odd. Consisting of a good-looking man who could not play his bass, a glam rocker Keith Richards-clone who'd been in half a dozen failed rock groups, and an old bloke who said he hated hippies but clearly had been one, The Clash dressed like poor people, played an incoherent sort of rock music with no love songs that seemed to do nothing but boast about how poor and unhappy they were, and occasionally played reggae, a kind of music that seemingly had nothing at all to do with punk rock. They didn't seem to fit in anywhere.

Nowadays we accept every kind of music. Guns 'N' Roses appeal to presidents, drum 'n' bass is used to announce the arrival of royalty at functions, Metallica record with orchestras and old ladies routinely buy Nine Inch Nails CDs. In 1976, however, nice people liked nice music and only the sick, insane and mentally crippled underclass of scum and murderers liked punk. This was an era when people had finally got used to long-haired youths, who were OK if they washed their hair every night. The hippy liberal consensus was starting to kick in. Then punk came along, which was totally opposed to consensus and niceness and happiness.

Punk was routinely hated by most people in its early months. Student unions managed to ban The Clash from playing because they thought 'White Riot' was racist. Local town and city councils managed to ban The Clash from playing because they thought they were anarchists. And the media and press just disliked the band because no one could play their instruments properly.

When The Clash began to get popular, they were liked. At the beginning of 1976 they had become one of the best live bands in Britain, if not the world. The energy and emotion that came off their shows was undeniable; their songs had sharp, witty lyrics and were even melodic. They were clearly very good and their rhetoric was appreciated by audiences, who really did want a people's band singing about their lives, who believed that The Clash were young idealists, and who could see not only that a change was very definitely going to come, but that this would be a good thing. These were not cynical times; and it was easy to see that The Clash were sincere people, even if Joe Strummer didn't look the 23 he claimed to be. Besides, these men were not Genesis, and in 1977 not being Genesis was good enough for most people. The Clash were taken on face value as honest, committed radicals who wanted to change the world and could be implicitly trusted.

Naturally – and this is one of the many Clash ironies – all these things conspired against the band when they had to put their money where their punk rock mouths were. Having campaigned, as it were, on a platform of honesty, Joe Strummer had to admit that he had lied about a few things: his age, and his name, and his education. Having made promises about integrity and wanting to change the system, The Clash signed to a huge record label for a large advance and apparently released records and used producers when CBS told them to.

Having said that they hated the boring old fart bands who

lost touch with their British audience, The Clash proceeded to spend all their time in America. In fact, having announced that they were bored with the USA and by implication promising to always be faithful to jealous old Britain, The Clash became so besotted with America that it was almost embarrassing. Previously, British bands had done well in America, members of The Beatles and The Rolling Stones even living there, but no one had dressed up as an American cowboy or soldier, written about the US or had their picture taken in America quite as much as The Clash would.

The Clash and America is one of the great love stories, *Romeo and Juliet* between a four-piece rock group and a huge nation state. It was a relationship that would eventually be consummated, to both parties' delight, but The Clash's relationship with America was a complicated one, and one that caused the band no end of grief. Famous for one song which offered a highly critical vision of the USA – 'I'm So Bored With The USA' – and made America appear to be a land of bad television, endemic violence, political corruption and general stupidity, The Clash then proceeded to do everything in their power to make friends with the USA. They signed to an American label; they hired an American producer for their second album; they covered an old American hit, 'I Fought The Law'; and they even sounded American on large parts of *London Calling. Sandinista!* and *Combat Rock* are full of the USA, and this is not entirely a result of the fact that the band were living in New York. Finally, The Clash became a big touring group in the USA, nothing more or less than a Rolling Stones for the early 1980s, and America loved them.

British people – who were, essentially, the band's fan base – did not love The Clash for this. Brits traditionally suspect success and certainly resent the fame of anyone who used to be theirs or who they could once see in a pub for a shilling. The Clash had to wait a long time before they were re-accepted by British fans. American fans, of course, do not care about this sort of thing.

The Clash, however, eventually became outsiders the way any person who outgrows their teenage years does. In 1976 The Clash were the new thing, young men with a new sound. In 1982, they were older and over-familiar. When the 1980s kicked in with new youth cults – 2-Tone and dance-oriented New Romantics in the manner of Duran Duran – The Clash seemed like a hangover from a previous generation, which in a sense they were. Most punk bands hadn't made it out of the 1970s; here it was 1982 and The Clash were still banging on about knowing your rights and the Vietnam War, while seemingly living an exciting life in New York. When the band split up, most people felt relief that The Clash had finally been put to sleep. When Strummer revived the band with The Clash Mark II, everyone found a smidgeon of optimism and hoped that maybe it would be good again. It was, but it wasn't good enough and so everyone just wanted Joe Strummer to shut up and go away, which, to his eternal credit, he did, burying himself in other projects for 15 years until people were interested in him again.

Cynics often ask what The Clash really achieved – as though they had planned to build a hospital or adopt a little donkey – and noted that by 1982 all The Clash had done was break America, and who cares about America, apart from rednecks and college kids? Cynics fail to notice that The Clash – for all their absurd posturing, increasing musical dullness and general decline – managed to do what no other British band with any wit or intelligence have managed to do since the 1960s, namely take their music to America and make it popular without any huge compromise.

Some bands – Ireland's U2 (who must give thanks every day that The Clash's departure left a stadium-sized hole for them to slip into), England's Bush – and some artists – Eric Clapton and Sting – broke America, and became very big; yet these acts were either playing a very American music already, or adapted their sound to the USA. None of them have ever done much that's fun or exciting after their American impact. Yet on *London Calling,* The Clash managed to sell reggae to America, on *Sandinista!* they sold an insane but thrilling ramble, and even on the dessicated *Combat Rock,* there was intelligence and humour. This at a time when 'new wave' didn't even mean Elvis Costello, it meant Linda Ronstadt doing bad versions of Elvis Costello songs. Joe Strummer always had a very strong desire to make The Clash's music known around the world, and while that music wasn't always good, it was always original and it made significantly fewer compromises than we are led to expect. A song like 'Straight To Hell' being on a top five American album would have been unthinkable before The Clash.

One of the great idiocies of British bands is that they go to America and play two cities – generally New York and Los Angeles – and then come home. The Jam played New York, got scared and gave up on America forever. Some bands try to tour the country, but get broken by the size and the repetition (in 1996 Oasis might have done very well in America, had Liam Gallagher not thrown a sulk and come home). The Clash worked America like an American band. If they ever professed to be a people's band, they had to now; for this was not music purely aimed at a few critics, but music for all. And no other group before the 1990s has been so multiracial in their tastes; The Clash brought hip hop and reggae to millions of white people, many of whom refused to listen until the well-rehearsed moronism of The Beastie Boys made it all right to like black music if no actual black people were involved in making it. The Clash introduced millions to black music and black acts.

The Clash embraced many contradictions, generally by accident, but one they were always, ultimately, very good with was America. They were never bored with the USA; and the USA repaid them by never being bored with The Clash.

Of course, some people say this was because The Clash were a trad-rock band born to be liked by Americans. Their best record, *London Calling*, was seen by some as a traditionalist's cop-out, an album of old-fashioned rock songs which would help the band in the USA (which it did) and which lacked the imagination and newness of the latest British bands (which it didn't). In 1978 and 1979, as The Clash looked to two very standard 1970s musical forms – hard rock and rock 'n' roll – for inspiration, new bands like Joy Division, Gang Of Four and Magazine were inventing a kind of music that genuinely had little to do with Elvis, The Beatles or The Rolling Stones. The Clash would always be secret Chuck Berry fans, and, while Chuck Berry is in reality one of the greatest recording artists of all time, in 1978 liking his music was similar to liking fourteenth-century monks' chants. The Clash liked music that your elder brother liked, because, essentially, they were your elder brother. So, incidentally, were The Stranglers, but they were so uncool and rancid that no one cared, and thus bought their records by the crateload.

In fact, The Clash were among the more inventive punk bands, because they quickly moved on from The Ramones' kind of punk. Where bands like The Sex Pistols, Sham 69 and, for three albums, The Ramones themselves stayed very true to the punk thrash, The Clash found themselves unable to continue down that line. *Give 'Em Enough Rope* is poor, you feel, because The Clash found themselves expected to repeat the first album, but they could and would not. The relief of *London Calling* – the sense of freedom that The Clash can do what they want and not listen to the punk orthodoxists – is clearly audible. Of course, after that, things went a little haywire, but not before The Clash had established themselves as imaginative and exciting.

The great irony of The Clash Mark II, by the way, is that they made the kind of punk rock – shouty, football terracey, simplistic, crude – that The Clash had never gone in for, even in their earliest days.

All good punk bands stopped being punk quite quickly by either splitting up or changing. It was easier to split up – then you could claim, as Neil Young said about Johnny Rotten, that it's better to burn out than to fade away – but changing was more rewarding. In real life Johnny Rotten understood this very well: he became John Lydon, formed Public Image Limited and made some of the most extraordinary music of his, or anyone else's, career.

When time moved on, The Clash went back to their template, but their template was both a rich historical one (all that American music) and an evolving one. Some of their efforts at rap may sound silly now, but amazingly some still work and no other band played rap *and* dub *and* rock and came out the victor. They may not have been very good at reggae when they started but they invented a musical form that allowed Sting to become rich. They may have only made one great rap record (no, not 'This Is Radio Clash') but it was an extraordinarily good one, which is genuinely funny. And they may have ensured that their various support acts, from electric minimalists Suicide and early hip-hopper Futura 2000 to Tex-Mexer Joe Ely, were regularly layered in mucus and lager by furious audiences eager to hear nothing new, but The Clash were at least trying to introduce new music to their audience.

The Clash were one of the few rock bands ever to be run on any kind of set of principles, no matter how silly or naive they may have been. There are few other bands with ideologies, unless they're stupid and pointless ones like Marilyn Manson or Kid Rock (Kid Rock may, of course, have a manifesto, but it probably smells of beer farts). The Clash had manifestos by the barrel, partly because Joe Strummer has always been a motormouth ideas man who was never afraid to not be cool, and partly because The Clash were, from time to time, a very principled band.

There are two problems with being a principled rock group. One is that once you've told everyone what your principles are – democracy, fairness, not ripping people off, and so on – if you then do something that contradicts your principles, people get very huffy and accuse you of hypocrisy. This is a little unfair, as bands with no principles, like Kiss and Hootie & The Blowfish, can get away with murder, or at the very least, boring people for years, and no one can say a word about it.

The other thing about principles is that the people with them can get very fond of being principled. It's part of the punk myth that bands cared about anything other then sex and beer; before punk, a group might sneak fans through a window or let them sleep on a hotel floor, but it took punk to make this part of the manifesto. Before punk, bands might do cheap shows or benefit concerts, but it was punk that fetishised this and made it into a myth. The Clash – much, much more than any other punk group – were a People's Band, group and audience united together, us and them against the world.

There are many, many Clash myths, some of them true: the time they gave a Cadillac to a town of unemployed people; the time their roadie attacked a top producer; the time their road manager threw their equipment in the Thames; the time Strummer got attacked by rock 'n' roll-loving teddy boys; the chair-removing at the Rainbow; the night Strummer played his radio to the audience; the story of 'Remote Control'; the story of *London Calling* and *Sandinista!* and the contracts; the mini-riots in Times Square; the pigeon-shooting incident and the trip to Jamaica. But, being The Clash, of course, they weren't content to sit back and let other people notice how mythic they were: The Clash wrote songs about it. From 'Garageland' (we are a garage band and defy the oppressor) to 'Clash City Rockers' (we are The Clash and you're not), from 'Cheapskates' (we have had badly paid jobs) and 'Guns On The Roof' (we have been victims of the police state) to 'Stay Free' (we have rough friends in jail) to 'All The Young Punks (New Boots And Contracts)' and 'Last Gang In Town' (we are even outsiders in the punk rock movement), The Clash could not stop writing songs about themselves. *London Calling's* 'Death Or Glory' and 'Four Horsemen' (we will die being a band/we are eternal figures as a band) took things into the realms of silliness, and even at the death, the Clash Mark II offered the simplest self-defining song: 'We Are The Clash'(and several nations' record buyers turned as one and said 'No You Are Not').

The Clash were more self-obsessed than Bo Diddley, than Ice-T, than even The Artist Formerly Known As Prince, whose 'My Name Is Prince' is probably the least new-information-containing single ever. The only band who have ever come close to them in self-love terms are Mott The Hoople, the Guy Stevens-produced band who nearly split up until David Bowie gave them 'All The Young Dudes' and then proceeded to write lots of songs about themselves, the best being 'Saturday Gigs', a farewell single which describes their entire career in three minutes.

Mott The Hoople were very much the proto-Clash, in rock terms, and the most Mott-like Clash song is 'Death Or Glory' – a very silly song indeed – but one which does contain the ultimate Clash line: 'He who fucks nuns will later join the church'. Joe Strummer knew all about contradictions, and The Clash were beset by so many contradictions that it seemed amazing they even stayed together for as long as they did. They tried to release a single every month but the record company wouldn't let them. They tried to release a four-track EP at a low price, but CBS made them charge extra for it. They wanted to start a club, or a radio station, or do cheap shows, but somehow they never got round to it. They were at their most political when Britain had a benign Labour government, but all their fury and rage seemed to have evaporated when Margaret Thatcher's genuinely hardline right-wing government came to power, by which time The Clash seemed more concerned with the politics of Nicaragua or America or even, fantasyland calling, Vietnam. And in the end people might pay to see Sylvester Stallone or Martin Sheen playing 'Nam vets or Saigon losers, but they weren't going to pay to see The Clash play-act.

The greatest contradiction for many Clash fans was the occasion of their signing to CBS. While no one had much cared when The Sex Pistols had done it – the Pistols were anarchistic rather than political and had, after all, managed to take EMI and A&M for a lot of money – The Clash had seemed to be the people's band who didn't care for fame and wealth. By signing to a huge multi-national, famous for pop acts like Simon & Garfunkel and Abba, The Clash seemed to be trading in their principles for a large sum of money, namely £100,000.

'The Clash sold out when they signed to CBS,' huffed fanzine editor Mark Perry, in an echo of John Lennon's equally disillusioned line, 'Elvis died when he went into the Army', and it's a typical Clash paradox that the band who set themselves up the most as principled outsiders would end up on a big fat capitalist label. It's to The Clash's credit that they understood the contradictions but they could never win.

'Complete Control' – a song about being forced to release a single by the record company, released by the record company they were criticising – may be the most ironic record ever made. It's less to their credit that the band never properly answered Perry's criticism, although Strummer weakly asked why Perry couldn't fight his own battles and Simonon observed that Perry had become a company director (albeit of a tiny indie label). The Clash were riled because they had been caught out, but so much of their best work was tied up in contradictions. They may have been a touch hypocritical, but let's face it, if The Clash had been perfect, you'd have wanted to smack them, not buy their records.

From being the people's punk band, The Clash went on to become the punk traitors, the band who failed to live up to the idealists' standards. Despite this – well, because of it – they were the inspiration for every political group who followed them. Not so much for their music: the influence of The Clash was immediate – hundreds of bands formed in their wake – but most found them a hard act to follow, preferring to go for the idiot thud of Sham 69. Even today, American bands like Rancid and The Offspring are more part of Britain's dim – if genuinely working-class – Oi! tradition, which had dubious right-wing roots and assumed that pretending to be a thug meant you were of the people. The Clash's influence – apart from giving Sting the idea of playing reggae – was more one of thought. The Clash wrote better social-comment lyrics than anyone else, and many bands picked up on this, from The Specials to Billy Bragg. If the 1980s killed political comment in music, The Clash's lyrics on their records kept some of that spirit alive. Now everyone is making their Clash tribute albums and raving about The Clash, but for a time they were a forgotten influence, buried under the horror of Simple Minds and Billy Idol and the dullness of '80s rock, (as opposed to '80s pop, which was great).

In many ways, 'influence' is a tricky word to use when talking about The Clash. Ironically, for a great punk band whose music is revered and shouted about by millions of other musicians, The Clash have influenced very few bands musically, even in England (The Redskins, anyone? Chumbawamba? Exactly). This is because their music was so idiosyncratic and distinctive that they were a musical cul-de-sac. Unlike other English punk bands, chiefly the horribly influential Sham 69 (themselves an English social realist and witless – literally – version of The Ramones), the Goth-inventing Siouxsie & The Banshees and The Jam (a revival of the superior Who), The Clash were a closed groove. And in America, where their musicianly nature put off young DIY punks, The Clash's only major effect on the punks there was the idea that you could be a rock group who played reggae and ska.

Both bouncy punks Rancid (whose Tim Armstrong owns the Hellcat label who signed Joe Strummer & The Mescaleros before anyone else) and jaunty popsters No Doubt have a lot of Clash in them in this respect. Rancid have worked with The Specials and The Mighty Mighty Bosstones (a band who feature on the *Burning London* tribute), while No Doubt's 'Just A Girl' is a song The Selecter would kill to have written: not that that's saying much, but the point is, for many US punks, The Clash are the band who did 'Rudie Can't Fail'.

Essentially, The Clash's influence on punk in America was both political and social. After the early nihilism of The Dils and The Germs died out (literally in the case of Germs singer Darby Crash, a Kurt Cobain for the 1970s whom hardly anyone has ever heard of), the second generation US punk bands took The Clash's route and developed social conscience. Thus, The Dead Kennedys may sound like the worst Leicester punk band, fronted by a duck, but they were more concerned with changing society. From Rancid to Green Day, American post-punk bands have been as interested in social action as social change.

Grumbly old British punks have a tendency to sneer at acts such as The Offspring and Green Day, while comparing them unfavourably to second division Britpunk bands The Members and The Ruts, but the fact remains that, so far as achievement and political thought go, American punk bands – with their general commitment to grass-roots issues, publicising left-of-centre causes and social comment lyrics – have taken on more Clash-influenced idealism than any British punk bands (and if that list includes The Clash, then such is the irony of history. Even The Clash were less influenced by The Clash than the American punk bands were).

The Clash, in any meaningful sense of the term, were the first popular band to play political rock music, and if they were full of contradictions, they inspired others to try harder.

In the 1980s British house fans thought that Chicago-spawned acid house was so called because everyone involved with it took LSD, when in fact they called it acid because the tracks burned like acid. British acid house was thus a lot druggier, hippier and brighter than the American version, all because of a misunderstanding. And so it was with The Clash. Strummer, Jones and Simonon may not have been real anarchists, they may not have known much about politics, and they almost certainly named an album *Sandinista!* because it sounded romantic rather than to show a deep understanding of CIA/US involvement in Nicaragua, but they gave people the idea that a rock band could be political.

The Clash invented something that simply had not existed before: the political rock band. Previously, protest music had, broadly speaking, been folk music. It implied that to attack the state, you had to like acoustic guitars, coffee bars and slow, plodding Bob Dylan-type melodies. It also implied, for the left, that electric guitars were somehow corrupting, and that liking rock music meant you were personally employed as an FBI informer.

The Clash – who have been described as a folk band, and there's some truth in that – put The Sex Pistols' nihilism and anarchy into real life, wrote about specific areas rather than vague blathering, and, most importantly of all, inspired a generation of bands. When punk left London, or New York, it stopped being a fashion statement and became a variety of different things, some of which were ideological. Bands like Crass, Flux of Pink Indians and Chumbawamba tried to take on the contradictions The Clash had failed to resolve – and in doing so became the precursors to the traveller protest movement, while in the USA, groups from Dead Kennedys to Rage Against The Machine asked what it was like to be a popular rock band and still genuinely oppose the status quo. People were inspired by The Clash not for what they actually achieved, but for what The Clash thought they might achieve. It's the idea of The Clash that's exciting, not just the music.

Mick Jones might have been less political, but Joe Strummer was one of the first artists to come out with lines like 'You can't live without politics.' He also originated one of the great punk sayings – 'Like Trousers, Like Brain' – which encapsulates punk's politics (attitude, arrogance and wit) brilliantly.

Pants apart, people who criticise The Clash for political hypocrisy are missing the point. For a start, criticising The Clash for not being proper poor people is like criticising The Rolling Stones for not being black blues singers; it's the result that matters here, not the motive. And the result was extraordinary. Who cares if CBS loved 'Complete Control'? It was still a fantastic beginner's guide to real-life politics and loss of innocence. So what if Joe Strummer talks in embarrassing Jamaican patois? Without his obsession with West Indian culture, we'd never have had '(White Man) In Hammersmith Palais'. And if, ultimately, The Clash tended to boast rather too much about how they were the first white rappers, or forget to mention that when they played Shea Stadium, they weren't actually the headliners, or claim that *Sandinista!* was an incredibly exciting experiment, rather than a lazy, failed contract-busting indulgence, who can blame them? The Clash always wanted to be a myth first and a band after, and so did everyone else.

The Clash will not be coming back, even if they make the terrible mistake of re-forming. Their time and place were the late 1970s, and when the 1980s began, The Clash had to go. With nostalgia for the band so big at the moment, it's hard to remember that people could actually get fed up with bands like The Clash. Unlike in the present day, when a record company will advise an act to leave an 18-month or two-year gap between CDs, and the act will do it, in the late 1970s and early '80s, bands released records every few months. The anticipation involved in waiting for a new Clash record palled rather when there was one out every week, and the bastard things kept getting longer and longer, and despite the high chart placings in Britain and America, *Combat Rock* was correctly seen as another musical disappointment at the time. This, coupled with the farce of The Clash Mark II and the rise of the new breed – REM, The Smiths, U2 – meant that The Clash were not missed in the 1980s. Only Mick Jones caught the mood of the era with his dance- and sample-heavy Big Audio Dynamite.

It was nice to see The Clash rewarded with a big hit when 'Should I Stay Or Should I Go?' finally hit big in 1991. And it is, as they say, very Clash that their only Number One single should be the music from a Levi's advertisement. It seems appropriate that the band who wouldn't do some televised pop shows, who spurned commercialism but who loved everything American would end up having their biggest hit off the back of a commericial for black jeans. Like trousers, like brain, indeed. But that will do, Clash-wise. We have some of the videos and all of the albums. The Clash in the new millennium would be pointless. Now the men who used to charge round the stage full of amphetamines and vigour are a quarter of a century older. Not all of them have hair.

As with The Jam and Siouxsie & The Banshees, The Clash will surely stay unre-formed. They certainly don't seem in a hurry to get back. Strummer's bohemianesque lifestyle, combined with the royalties from soundtracks and reissues,

Jones's keenness to make new music and Simonon's success as a painter are all against it, as are the bad experience of The Clash Mark II and the band's reluctance – as with Led Zeppelin and, almost, The Who – to carry on without a fourth member (who, despite being the drummer, was an essential part of the mix) may well keep them apart.

True, they could go back to the studio, but why bother? In the 1990s, Strummer and Jones reunited to write a few songs for Big Audio Dynamite. The results, while good, were hardly essential. There are plenty of Clash records out there, videos, live bootlegs (for the obsessives), quite enough to be going on with. And if you like 'Rock The Casbah' that much, you can always buy that Will Smith album.

These days you can never say that a band won't get back together. Even The Beatles did it and one of them was dead. But it would be a bad idea indeed if The Clash did. 'Now we're gone,' sighs Paul Simonon wistfully but firmly in Don Letts's documentary *From Westway To The World*. And they really are.

In the end The Clash worked for two reasons; one was the moment they appeared. There have been few giant upheavals in British music – acid house was one, The Beatles another – and bands rarely do extraordinary things in isolation. Jones and Simonon would never have been inspired to go out and form something as radical as The Clash if punk rock had not been in the air, and if they had not seen or hung out with The Sex Pistols. Joe Strummer would never have walked out of The 101'ers, his own, moderately popular band, without the huge incentive of the opportunity to become involved with a totally different and radical new form of music that had never been tried before and had the power to fire up a musician in his late twenties. And Jones and Simonon would never have approached Strummer or worked with him at any other point in pop history.

There are other moments here, too. The Clash knew Bernie Rhodes, who was Malcolm McLaren's near-partner. They had not dropped in from nowhere, but had been in bands before, so knew their way around. The country was ready for some aggressive new music and The Clash played strange new songs and even reggae, at a time when reggae needed a white group to bring it overground post-Bob Marley; and, perhaps most significant of all later, America was bored and wanted a cool new rock band and didn't know it. But all of these variables pale into insignificance next to the one simple fact that The Clash were an extraordinary mix of personalities, and that it was the personalities involved who made the group what it was.

Paul Simonon could barely play his instrument, but this being punk, that didn't matter – he looked great, dressed imaginatively, and brought the image – Jamaican gangster, World War II American pilot, Ennio Morricone cowboy, general rock 'n' roll cool. Mick Jones was something of a throwback to a pre-punk kind of rock with his drugs and his posing, but he was the musician of the band and the rock fan who gave The Clash the arrogance and the speed all great rock bands need, as well as the tower-block credibility ('I hate the country. The minute I see cows I feel sick' he once said, brilliantly). And Joe Strummer may have been somewhat older than the rest, and always uncool, but he was the visionary, a man who talked a great fight slightly more than he talked nonsense, a street preacher and, on the right night, a shaman, the one who believed in the idea of The Clash more than anyone. Alone, these three people had done nothing much in music; together, they made an extraordinary rock group. 'The idea of the band was to play it maximum,' chirped Strummer once, and that's exactly what The Clash did.

For seven short and very fast years, The Clash – working all the time, talking all the time, having their picture taken all the time – invented new kinds of music, produced exciting, unbelievable records, said extraordinary things and went to places no bands had ever been to. In the end, they were, like all bands, doomed. Topper Headon's drug problems meant that an essential member of the band had to leave, causing the band to wobble and eventually implode. Strummer's constant rhetoric and urge to make myths and manifestos meant that sooner or later The Clash would cry wolf once too often and people would get fed up with them; Simonon, not a major musical contributor to the band, and with skills outside rock, would eventually get bored and want to pursue his other abilities: and Jones's rock-star attitude would not only provide a huge contrast between the way he lived and the way The Clash said life should be lived, but it would also drive a wedge between himself and the rest of the band. But for the relatively long period that The Clash were together, they managed to do, say and record more than most bands do in a century.

INDEX

PICTURE CREDITS